The Spanking Writers
Volume II

The best of the blog
2008-2009

Abel and Haron

The Spanking Writers
Abel and Haron

First published in Great Britain in 2010 by
Abelard Books
www.abelardbooks.co.uk

Copyright © Abel and Haron

A catalogue record for this book is available from the British Library

ISBN 978-0-9558483-3-9

The moral rights of the authors have been asserted. All rights reserved. No part of this publication may be reproduced, stored in a retrieval system or transmitted in any form or by any means, electronic, mechanical or otherwise without the written permission of the Publisher.

2008

Off to a spanking start

By Abel on 1 January 2008

Last night's New Year's Eve party at our Malaysian resort was rather ghastly, the otherwise excellent hotel management cynically exploiting their captive audience by charging disgracefully inflated sums for food that was no better than usual, a band that would shame a third-rate karaoke joint, and a CD of seventies disco classics.

Things looked up on the stroke of midnight, though, with a spectacular fireworks display, and before very long guests were welcoming 2008 by diving into the swimming pool in their posh frocks. The new year was therefore a mere quarter-hour old before it inspired its first kinky imaginings.

I pictured a giggling group of girls from the hotel staff diving in to join the fun, carried away by the spirit of the occasion into forgetting that they were still on duty. And then their supervisor appeared. Orders were barked;

bedraggled girls in hotel uniforms clambered, dripping out of the pool.

This morning, the General Manager's first duty of the new year was to deal with the miscreants – silent, nervous, regretful, downcast – lining the corridor outside his office. He'd leave the door open as he called them in, one by one, the sounds of their canings floating down the hallway to add to the lesson being learnt by their friends.

PS as to how any fathers might have dealt with daughters drenching designer dresses, I shall leave that entirely to your imaginations...

PPS 10.30am, across my knee as I sat on a sun lounger, if you were wondering when Haron's cheekiness first got her into trouble this year. The beach was pretty quiet, but she still seemed a little alarmed when I started to pull down her swimming costume...

Counting schoolgirls

By Haron on 14 January 2008

When you wake up in the middle of the night and can't go back to sleep, what do you do?

Mostly, I listen to audiobooks or podcasts on my iPod, but last night it was out of battery after a train journey. I had to resort to counting sheep.

Hang on, thought I, sheep? Why? I'd rather count something pleasant, that would carry me off to an interesting dream.

At first, I thought about counting cane strokes landing on a schoolgirl's bottom as she is bent over a trestle. Then the count got a little too high, my schoolgirl was getting too sore, and the fantasy needed adjustment.

I started simply counting schoolgirls as they walked past single-file, imagining each one in every detail. This didn't particularly work either, because I couldn't figure out where they were going in such great numbers, and this nagged me, and wouldn't let me go to sleep.

Finally I got onto the perfect solution.

I had the whole school lined up around a courtyard. This was an assembly following a major riot. In the middle there was a trestle.

Each schoolgirl was going to walk to the trestle, raise her skirt, bend over and receive six strokes of the cane from a gowned housemaster. I would count them to the middle, count the stroke, and carry on to the next girl.

This worked its calming wonders: I got through about fifteen girls and their stripes before I fell asleep. I still prefer my iPod, but now I'm well prepared for any future technical difficulties.

If you wish to try out this method and report back on your success, I'm sure we will all be interested in hearing how you get on!

Porn. With added stripes.

By Abel on 15 January 2008

A frank discussion with kinky friends recently concerned our early porn-reading days as teenagers. How I enjoyed some of those long summer holidays from school – parents safely out of the way, pocket money in hand and the local newsagent's top shelf just in reach!

It did seem that I had a rather unusual approach to my porn-reading, though. You see, browsing naughty magazines for me involved the use of a red pen. Pictures of delectable backsides soon became adorned with hand-drawn stripes, as I pictured the canings and whippings that the scantily-clad (nay, often completely unclad) young ladies would have received. "Readers' Wives" became "Spanked Readers' Wives"; "Penthouse" transmuted into "Jailhouse" and "Men Only" (a particular favourite) metamorphosed into "Strict Men Only".

And that was before I'd realised that I was kinky, or even what "kinky" was.

Selling her uniform

By Haron on 20 January 2008

The following dialogue occurred last week between Abel in London and me at home.

> Abel: Sat at the O2 surrounded by cuties going to the Spice Girls, about to eat in the "S&M cafe". I so want one of their waitress's uniforms...
>
> Haron: See if you can get a uniform off of a cutie for a few pounds. As a bonus, she'll have to go naked, and will also get a spanking from her manager for selling the uniform.

Some days I feel like apologising to Abel for creating the impression that *he* is the evil one here.

Caned by the Inspector: a scene

By Abel on 23 January 2008

I wonder whether young Martha's work colleagues noticed her squirming uncomfortably behind her desk the other morning? If so, then I must record my confession...

She'd emerged from her shower to find an Inspector from The Party's police force waiting in her dorm room. He enquired after one of her friends "since we are somewhat concerned for his welfare." Reluctantly, she confessed that she had been with the young man in question into the early hours of the morning.

The inspector was grateful for her confirmation of the former part of her friend's story; he challenged her with the latter. "Your Comrade tells me that during your time together, you made various disparaging remarks about the Party leadership, in direct violation of section 7.3 of Party rules. He therefore visited us this morning to notify us of the offence."

The girl knew the potential consequences, of course: fortunately for her, the Inspector seemed minded to be generous.

"Do you recall the punishment detailed in sub-section 15.3.2 of the rules for such an offence?" He paused momentarily, before continuing. "Comrade Martha, you may count yourself lucky that I do not this morning intend to impose the more serious punishment available to me, of stripping you of your Party membership. You will understand that that would inevitably result in you being expelled from the Party University."

"Thank you, sir."

"Instead, I will administer the lesser penalty of a thrashing. Can you recall, Comrade, the number of strokes of the cane specified for breaches of section 7.3?"

"Six, sir?"

"Between ten and fifteen. So I shall start by administering ten, and we shall then see whether you are suitably repentant, or whether I need to continue to the higher total."

—

So, dear readers, you will understand Martha's discomfort. The inspector applied the heavy dragon cane with some considerable vigour; one of the ten strokes had to be re-applied as the girl failed to take it appropriately.

When instructed to stand afterwards, her silence resulted in further punishment: "If you are not yet ready to express your remorse, then I shall see if two more strokes loosen your tongue."

And then it was time to leave for work, the young lady wincing all the way, much to my enjoyment.

Dreaming of the workhouse

By Abel on 28 January 2008

I cuddled up to Haron as she stirred yesterday morning, and whispered my night's dream to her.

I'd been a gentleman visiting the local Workhouse, to select a girl. Not for any illicit purposes, you understand: I needed a bright young thing to help with some work in my country house.

I'd interviewed a selection of their inmates: one girl stood out, shy but sharp. On payment of the appropriate fee, the Master of the Workhouse brought her to me. Only there was a slight hitch: "You see, sir, she's due a whipping at the end of the month with some of the other girls, and I'm not sure whether we should let her leave before then."

A compromise was reached. The flogging block was brought into the room, the trembling girl stripped naked and tied tightly down. I watched – she was my property now, after all – as the Punishment Officer did his harsh duty.

And after it was done, she was made to dress. The final signature was added to the paperwork, discharging her into my care; we journeyed home in my carriage, every bump in the road bringing fresh tears to her eyes.

From bad dream to worse reality

By Haron on 29 January 2008

As I was drifting off to sleep last night, I came awake with an involuntary jump.

"What happened? Did the bad men get you?" asked Abel.

"I fell off a tree," I complained. "I was stealing apples... and fell off."

"You were doing *what*? Bad girl: come here!" He swiftly turned me over onto my tummy and gave me several crisp smacks. "And that's just from the owner of the orchard. Wait till you come home, and your daddy whips you with his belt."

I wouldn't put it past Abel to get out of bed and fetch an implement, but luckily it was too cold outside our nice duvet, and we were too tired. So instead we fantasised.

...The girl would be too scared to go home after being discovered; this was a small town, and daddy would surely find out. She would wander the streets for a while, and then spend the night at her friend's house.

Only, she couldn't avoid going home forever. Her father would meet her silently by the door, where he would hand her his pocket knife, and motion towards the trees in the yard.

Under the curious gazes of the neighbours she would cut a switch for her whipping. An apple switch for an apple thief.

The commander's daughter

By Abel on 11 February 2008

An advert for a hotel spa near Hadrian's Wall spun me back in time. It was the Roman era, in the bath house on the same site. The beautiful daughter of the legion's commander walked in, letting her toga slip to the floor, revealing the fresh stripes of a sound whipping.

But was she there of choice, determined to show that she was not ashamed: proud, defiant?

Or, rather, had her father sent her there – refusing to allow her to sob in her room, wanting the word to get out that he was as severe with his own daughter as he expected his officers to be with theirs?

Red-sealed envelope

By Haron on 12 February 2008

Coming home from a weekend away, I found a letter addressed to me by HM Revenue and Customs. I don't know if it's just me, but I quiver when I get these, despite my complete and transparent law-abidingness. Just that "private" stamp makes my stomach go floppity.

This particular letter said something along the lines of "Dear Haron, you've paid too much tax, please have some money back, you good girl you." In fact, I'd expected to get something like it. And still, I had to sit down before reading it.

If the tax man scares me so much, you can imagine how much I sympathise with the girls who get the letters with the official red seal of the Regional Correctional Office, also known as "the whipping man". Of course, they also know it's coming – they look out for it since the day they're sentenced for their petty crimes. And yet, when it's finally here – that simple, straightforward "Report for your flogging at this hour, at that place" – they can hardly bear to open it.

The flogging is deserved, of course. Still, I sympathise. They are never easy to unseal, those official-looking letters.

Writing lines

By Haron on 21 February 2008

My Valentine's Day gift from Abel was a set of new calligraphy pens, nibs and inks. Having not yet found a home for them, I keep them on the table next to my laptop. For some odd reason, the thoughts I have most frequently when I look at them are not about practising calligraphy, but about writing lines.

When I was a kid, it was the one type of punishment I could give to myself. It didn't get corrupted by my being unable to spank myself hard enough, or lacking a play-partner to physically interact with me. I could simply sit at my table and write lines, pretending I was at school.

As I think about this, I marvel at how diverse line-writing can be. You can use them in several different ways:

A punishment in themselves. (A naughty girl is given masses of them to write out in an evening. With a dip pen. When she could be reading or watching TV.)

An addition to spanking. (As above, but the naughty girl writes her lines with a tender bottom, or perhaps, with her hands sore from a strapping.)

A prelude for further punishment. (As above, but the top checks the sheet for neatness, mistakes and miscounts, allocating another spanking for these.)

I enjoy all three, though the third is my favourite. As long as the top can bring himself to be fair, and not pick on my writing excessively. Not that I'm implying that anybody ever would.

Which do you like best?

The lady and the maid
By Abel on 2 March 2008

Sometimes the framework of a spanking plot reveals itself clearly, but the detail is somewhat imprecise. The gentleman in my dreams – the lord of some manor – had caught his young lady with her maid, both stark naked, indulging in the most unspeakably intimate of acts.

The maid would be sent to stand to the side of the room, to watch as he reached for the riding crop and thrashed his charge particularly thoroughly, whilst she bent over the foot of the four-poster bed. And then the master would ring the bell to summon the butler, and demand that the maid be taken downstairs and whipped most soundly.

Only I can't quite work out – would his young lady be a daughter, a ward (sent to his care by some grateful relative) or his wife?

Schoolgirl for the weekend
By Haron on 6 March 2008

As far as my spanking fetish is concerned, I've got two absolute favourite things: being a schoolgirl, and role-playing complicated, drawn-out scenes. Mix the two together, and you get a happy Haron in a state of kinky bliss.

Abel and I were lucky enough to spend last weekend participating in the longest, most immersing school role-play experience either of us had ever tried: a boarding school, complete with lessons, assemblies, chapel, school play, dorm inspections, games and homework. Oh, and spankings for the girls who misbehaved.

Describing the whole thing would turn any blog post into a novel (and would do nasty things to other people's privacy), but I can't resist posting some highlights – the bright pictures flashing up in my memory's eye.

1. Each girl carries a "points book", wherein her achievements and misdeeds are recorded. During a lesson Abel demands to see mine. I toss it across the room at him, marvelling at my own audacity. Pause. With a cold voice, he orders me to get out of his classroom. There are only a few minutes of the lesson left, but this is enough for several other masters to wander on the way to and from their bedrooms. Each gives me a knowing look. My housemaster walks past. "Why are you here, girl?" I explain, cringing. He simply says, "Mmm-hmm." I expect to hear about this again at the house meeting later in the evening. The noise level in the classroom rises as Abel emerges, cane in hand. Bent over a chair with my skirt up, I receive three sharp, measured strokes. I can't help jumping up after each one. This is my first punishment of the "school term", and it remains the most painful.

2. We are not allowed to ask for anything at meals; we must wait to be offered. Thus, if we are to have any hope to get fed ourselves, we should look out for our neighbours' needs, and practice heavy hinting. "Would you like some orange juice?" you ask a girl whose glass is full of water. It takes her two seconds to twig it, and then – "No, thank you, but would you like some yourself?" "Why, yes please, how kind of you to ask!"

3. Some of the girls have university degrees in the subjects that are taught, but we are careful not to be too clever. Nobody wants to earn too many points to get spanked later. All the same, the behaviour is mostly unbelievably good. At one point the master sets a task and leaves for a good five minutes. There is no mischief, no conversations, nobody throws paper planes or gets out

the pea-shooters. He comes back to find an impeccable classroom. (The only miscreant being yours truly, caught reading a book for the next lesson under the desk. But I'd finished my task, what can I say!)

4. There are two houses, five girls in each. We have our assemblies in the evening. The housemaster and the junior master attached to the house examine our points books. One girl is praised and dismissed, the rest are sent to queue for their punishment outside. We end up huddling on a tiny landing. I'm the second to go in, but after my punishment (consisting of a spanking, a surprise mouth-soaping earned on the spot, and eight of the best), I linger to the end, offering and receiving comfort from the others. We can hear the other house assembly finish, and our dinner being served, but we wait in the dark, shell-shocked. We are the naughtiest of the naughty.

5. Abel has inspired me to a piece of naughtiness I would never have perpetrated on my own. Visiting Blackpool several days previously, we happened upon a shop selling sticks of rock (local traditional sweets) inscribed with messages, from names to insults. We bought five pieces saying "Pervert", and I conspired with the kitchen staff for these to be served to the teachers with their whisky in the staffroom. In assembly, the Headmaster demands that the guilty party owns up. I'm so deep in a schoolgirl head that my tongue freezes in my mouth: I don't dare speak up. I think better of it almost immediately, but the moment for confession is gone. All morning I go through options in my head. I don't want to go to the Head. Could I go to my personal tutor? Or ask the kitchen boy who had helped me to snitch on me? In the end, I do go to straight to the Headmaster, who coldly orders me to his office in break. I arrive there fresh from a caning from my housemaster for an unrelated offence, but

I can't handle putting this off. I get a spanking, a good dose of leather paddle, and a dozen with the cane to sink the message in. The punishment itself is not the harshest ever, but the lecture is so crushing that I leave in tears.

This is as much as I'm comfortable writing without giving away anything somebody may want to keep secret. I hope that those of my playmates who happen to read this might consider adding their own experiences in the comments. You are all most welcome to reminisce with me. In fact, I hope you do!

Bottom of the class
By Haron on 10 March 2008

When Abel came home for the weekend, I reminded him that my guardian still hadn't dealt with me for coming bottom of the class over our school weekend. (Although I was surprised to have done so badly, I was happy to exploit the situation. And why not?)
   Funnily enough, he didn't need much convincing. We had a little chat about what we thought the history was between me and my guardian. We established that, although he had never spanked me before, last time I came bottom of the class he had promised me a caning if I didn't shape up. And here I was again, not at all improved.
   I did try to argue, when, standing in front of him in his office, I was faced with his reproaches. I said that, to my mind, I was very much improved. It was only that the other girls had also improved, and because my position was dependent on how other girls scored, it was unfair to punish me for their improvement. Did that impress my guardian? Not in the least.

He made me stand in the corner while he shuffled the furniture and picked an implement behind me. Trying to impress him with how good I was, I didn't peek at all, even though I was dying to know which cane he had chosen. Finally, he told me to bare my bottom and bend over the chair.

"How many times have you been caned this term?" he asked.

This was a very hard question. I was glad he didn't ask how many times I was punished, because there had been so many random smacks, swats and licks of the strap, I would never have remembered them all.

"Um, about five?" I guessed. (Probably wrong, but best I could do under the circumstances.)

"And what was the biggest number of strokes you received?"

"Twelve, sir." I knew that. I remembered each one.

"Very well. I will give you the same number. You will count them and thank me."

I couldn't believe how much the first stroke hurt. The office is quite narrow, and doesn't have much swinging space, so I just wasn't prepared for the overwhelming pain that suddenly assaulted me. I was struggling by the fifth stroke. It was only my guardian's mercifully quick delivery of the last several strokes that helped me get through it. If I was the crying sort, I would have been sobbing.

"You may get up and adjust your clothing," he said curtly. I did, sniffling, and dancing on the spot as my previously comfy soft trousers brushed past my injured parts.

"Stop these dramatics, young lady, you are used to being caned," said my evil guardian.

I nearly burst out laughing at the idea that you can somehow *get used* to being caned. If I were a cheeky sort, I would have suggested that he cut his finger every week for a year, to see whether it started hurting less the more he did it. However, I decided I'd been punished enough, so I meekly said: "You can't get used to it, sir." I don't think he believed me.

After I was dismissed, we had our after-scene cuddles, and I finally asked to see the cane he had used. Well, no wonder it had hurt: it's a very short, very thick, unbelievably stiff piece of wood. More of a swagger stick than a cane. However, it didn't need to be swung very high, which was, apparently ideal for the cramped office conditions.

I would probably burn it, if I didn't suspect some of our friends would rather enjoy making its acquaintance.

I will tell you one thing: if by some unfortunate accident I will come bottom of the class again at a future school gathering, I'm not seeing my guardian afterwards. I don't want to find out what he might do to me next time!

At the Victorian workhouse

By Haron on 17 March 2008

On Saturday evening, inspired by the Victorian spirit of Beamish Museum, we girls found ourselves transforming into inhabitants of a strict workhouse.

Rapunzel became Rose, a poor orphan; Martha remained Martha, but became a young delinquent, caught pilfering biscuits from a shop, and I was Louise, and had had to be committed to the workhouse following my destitute mother (who had ended up in a different section).

All three of us had been chosen by the master of the workhouse, Mr Jenkins, to serve dinner to a visiting chairman of the governors, Sir Ashley Piers. We were supposed to make the best impression on the distinguished visitor, so that he continued to provide charitable support to our establishment, and perhaps even increased the funding. He was also looking to employ the best-behaved girl at his London residence. Although I felt a momentary wistful twinge, I could predict that by the end this would not be me.

Sir Ashley arrived just before the bathing hour, as we girls were lined up in front of the bathhouse, our modesty covered with nothing but the towels we were clutching. Mr Jenkins and Sir Ashley supervised our baths, making sure we cleaned ourselves properly with lukewarm water and carbolic soap, as we would be serving their food and joining them for dinner. Rose and I managed to get through the experience without invoking their wrath, but poor Martha had to endure a spanking when the gentlemen noticed her painted toenails. (A sign of bad character, I think.)

Although we were hoping to be allowed to dress right away, Sir Ashley had a surprise in store for us. He told Mr Jenkins about an interesting practice in other workhouses, where girls got a weekly dose of discipline after their baths. Apparently, a spanking a week improved overall behaviour, and made sure the girls didn't misbehave at other times, thus earning harder punishments.

First of all, to demonstrate the technique and the necessary severity, Sir Ashley took me over his knee, and delivered a not-too-hard, but still quite stingy spanking. Although I'd done my best to dry off properly after my bath, my skin was still slightly moist, and quite cool from the chilly water, so I whimpered and wriggled quite a lot. That said, when Sir Ashley told me to stop carrying on so much, I tried hard to make a good impression and to take the discipline bravely.

Rose and Martha then received their own spankings. The girls who were not being spanked at the time had to stand in the corridor facing the wall, so I can't say much about the severity of what they had to endure. I know, however, that Mr Jenkins tried his hand at this new style of discipline as well, and at some point a hairbrush was brought out when his palm began stinging too much to continue.

Finally, the gentlemen retreated, allowing us to dress in our workhouse uniforms. (Rapunzel had brought along three black dresses with white lacy cuffs, which looked like something Orphan Annie would wear.) We hurried downstairs to see to the meal (for the most part prepared in advance, with only some finishing touches and serving necessary).

The girls may wish to speak for themselves in the comments, but I for one went very deep into the head of Louise. She was a meek girl, deeply grateful for the chance to impress a visitor. Any sort of deliberate mischief was out of the question: I really wanted to show the workhouse in the best light, to earn the praise of the master, and to help secure the extra funding from the governor. Thus, any mistakes I made were entirely accidental, and I was genuinely grieved to have earned six strokes of the cane by the time the meal was over. To make my downfall slightly less crushing, the other two girls couldn't help making mistakes either, so all three of us were due a caning by the end.

I was sent to fetch a cane, and to wait naked for my punishment while Martha received her own six strokes. Rose waited with me. She was visibly nervous: she hoped to be hired by Sir Ashley as a maid in his London residence, and she was worried that her mistake would hurt her chances. I was sure that this wouldn't happen, as throughout the dinner Rose showed herself the best of the three of us, keeping up small-talk, and displaying impeccable manners while Martha and I fumbled and stuttered. Surely, a caning wouldn't imperil my friend's chances.

I hated leaving her alone and shivering in the corridor, but Sir Ashley arrived to administer my punishment. He was not unduly harsh, as he must have recognised that any mistakes I'd made were not at all deliberate. The cane stung, but I was able to take it more or less bravely. Sir Ashley praised me for this, and promised that the workhouse would indeed not close, but would receive the extra funding we were all hoping for. I think we girls had made the right impression.

We learned afterwards that Rose was indeed hired by Sir Ashley, and would be leaving with him for London the following day. This was just as well, really, as I don't imagine Rapunzel would have wanted to stay in our house forever :-)

Restless in the reformatory

By Abel on 21 March 2008

Haron was restless the other night – my habit of sleeping with the window open isn't always that helpful when the north-east temperatures plunge towards freezing. I started to dream of girls at a reform school, sent to bed at an early hour. The rules would be simple: if they were caught awake after a certain time, they would be caned.

A master wandered through a dorm; too late, a girl noticed him, and pretended to close her eyes. "Report to my study," he ordered, before continuing his inspection.

Through the chill, dark, empty corridors she crept, terrified. A caning was inevitable – her first in many months, since she'd vowed to stay clear of trouble. The memories of previous punishments came flooding back.

A long wait ensued outside his door. Was his tour of the dorms taking longer than usual? Had he forgotten her?

And then, in the distance, his footsteps, drawing nearer. As he approached, she felt herself cower. He showed her in: was brisk, to the point, already fetching down the cane as he explained that she knew the rules and knew the consequences. He made her lift her nightdress, touch her toes: the six strokes were harsh across her cold, bare backside.

At this point, I woke, and whispered details of the dream to Haron. And then the story developed some more as we cuddled. The master had ordered the girl return to the dormitory without further ado. But she'd taken a detour, curled up gingerly on some bench to compose herself. The reformatory headmaster appeared around the corner. Her heart leapt.

"What are you doing here?"

She murmured a panicked explanation: she'd got into trouble; she'd been caned; she was just catching her breath.

"But this isn't on the way back to your dorm from his study..."

"No, sir."

"Did he tell you to go directly back?"

"Yes, sir."

"Then you will follow me."

And he led her into an empty classroom, took the cane from the cupboard, made her remove her nightdress and bend over the front desk. "Six strokes clearly weren't sufficient to teach you the importance of obedience, young lady," he'd say. The pain of his first cut would make the other master's whacks feel like gentle caresses. By the time she'd taken all twelve she'd be sobbing for forgiveness.

And this time, when it was over, she *would* run straight back to the dorm, clambering into her bed and pulling the sheets over her lest the other girls saw her cry.

Catching the runaway

By Haron on 1 April 2008

The girl waiting on our table in a London cafe was sweet, cute and efficient, but extremely shy. Every time she came by to set down a piece of cutlery or a plate of food, she blushed and apologised with no real reason for either. "Sorry," she would say, putting down a napkin.

"I'm so sorry," there comes a cup of coffee.

I just wanted to scream: "It's okay! Honestly! Feeding us is fine, you don't have to apologise!"

Just as we set about demolishing our cake, a young man walked into the relatively empty cafe, and strode moodily to the bar. (In the interests of full disclosure I must say that he was extremely good-looking in an arrogant sort of way.) He showed no interest in ordering, and instead he leaned onto the counter, and stood there, silent and glaring, until our sweet waitress had a spare moment to come and talk to him. When she approached, he spoke to her in Portuguese, his tone harsh, his features frowning. She replied with a blush noticeable even from where we sat, and darted away to serve somebody with their coffee. He frowned, and waited for her to come free again.

This dance continued in front of us. She would spare a minute to talk to the guy, he would glare and growl, she would respond pleadingly, and flit away with a plate of food.

Not understanding any Portuguese, I had to supply my own story.

The moody guy was the girl's brother. She was supposed to be at home, studying at her local university. She had always wanted to travel and see the world, but her parents said she had to finish her degree first. Then, last Christmas, she announced she was going away with her girlfriends for a few days: a short hop over the border to Spain, that was all.

Except, when the girlfriends returned, she was not with them. Shamefaced, they reported to the girl's father that she had suspended her course at uni, and has gone travelling. None of them knew where exactly; she had carefully kept her plans to herself.

Not wishing to involve the police, the father hired a private detective, who carefully followed her trail as she travelled around Europe, taking on small jobs to keep cash coming in. Finally, after a few months, he discovered her in London, waiting tables in Soho by day and soaking up metropolitan life at night. The girl's brother was promptly dispatched to fetch her home without raising a scandal.

And here they were: the guy, watchful and seething, and the girl, stumbling and apologising to customers through her last minutes of freedom. "Don't try to slip away," were her brother's first words to her. "You're coming home." He put his hands on his waist, hooking his fingers into his belt, and she knew at once that she wouldn't dare defy him.

She was going home, to face her father's wrath.

The parable of the good and worthy girl

By Abel on 6 April 2008

I so enjoyed writing the Sunday morning sermon for the school role-play we so enjoyed a few weeks ago. With a mix of girls, some religious, some not, there was a fine line to tread lest I cause offence.

A spoof parable formed the basis of my preaching, and seemed to do the trick, and I can't resist publishing it here – rather than consigning it to the outer reaches of my laptop, never to see the light of day again.

It was taken from the (entirely non-existent) Book of Jonathan, chapter 6, verses 14 – 18:

> For the girl didst speak ill words to her father, and this pained her father, and he in turn pained her. "Dost thou not know to honour thine parents?" he spake, solemnly, before sending her out into the oasis to cut a switch from the apple tree that didst bless the family with its fruits.
>
> And he didst punish her severely, and the girl wast sorely chastened.
>
> It was but three moons later that the Feast of Archibald fell upon them, and as is set out by the scriptures, the young women of the village gathered in the temple to hear the Elders speak. Yet the girl didst not gather with the others at the anointed hour. She made her way tardily to the temple, and lo, she didst there gossip with another girl whilst the Elders taught.
>
> And the preacher became mightily annoyed. "Dost thou not know to honour thine Elders?" he spake, solemnly, before sending her to the front of the temple to bend over before the other girls, and taking out his rod.
>
> And he didst punish her severely, and the girl wast sorely chastened.
>
> It was but three weeks later that the girl wast riding a donkey through the village when she didst pass a fruit grove, full of the ripest, juiciest and most tasty pears imaginable. She tied her ass at the side of the track, and didst climb into the hidden orchard, gorging on the forbidden fruits.
>
> But lo, the fruit owner didst catch her, and didst take her before the judge. "Dost thou not know to honour thine neighbours?" he spake, solemnly, before sending her to the village square, and beseeching the local boys to make haste and cut a bundle of birches.
>
> And he didst punish her severely, and the girl wast sorely chastened.

And the girl returned home, and didst lie on her front on her bed, weeping. And as she wept, and reflected on the lessons that she had experienced, she vowed that she would be a good and worthy girl henceforth. And she became loved by all, and much praised, and lived happily until the age of four hundred and seventy three.

What's a tawse, please?

By Haron on 8 April 2008

The "Daily Mail" has a section called Answers to Correspondents. You write to them with your question, they publish it, and then publish responses sent in by other readers. Last week's page included a question:

> My father was at school in the Fifties and said there was not much bad behaviour because 'those who caused trouble would get six or twelve with the tawse.' What's a tawse?

I smelled a rat when I read this question. If the correspondent genuinely didn't know, why didn't he or she ask the father, rather than writing to a newspaper? I bet they were fishing for people's stories of childhood corporal punishment. Oh, the rascals.

The idea does lend itself to an interesting game: seeing what sort of outrageous question you can get into the newspaper.

> My granny said her governess used to spank her with a brush. I think it's outrageous, poor granny. Were all governesses allowed to do things like that?

Or

> My new boyfriend has a collection of solid ebony hairbrushes on his bedside table, but he is completely bald. Why are they there?

Or

I was going through airport security, and the man behind me set off the metal detector. He calmly explained that it was because of Prince Albert, and was allowed through. What does Queen Victoria's dead husband have to do with metal detectors?

OK, I've exhausted my supply of naughtiness for this morning. Would you like to have a go? Or, better yet, would you like to just send your questions to the papers, and see if you get in?

Tips for newbie caners

By Abel on 18 April 2008

One of our occasional commenters here at Spanking Writers wrote to us recently, with a plea. She'd just plucked up the courage to invest in some canes for the first time – and had realised that neither she, nor her husband, actually really knew how to apply a caning safely and effectively. Did I have any advice?

Being keen to ensure that the canes didn't gather dust in the cupboard for lack of suggestions, I threw together a quick twelve-of-the-best tips for them to consider. I thought it'd be fun to post the list here – and to get others' comments on technique for newbie caners:

1. Practice first: get used to hitting the target by whacking pillows. (Yes, it may sound silly, but…)

2. Give a warm-up – say an OTK spanking first: it helps to make the cane strokes slightly more bearable (even though some think it's inauthentic if you're playing, say, a school scene).

3. Choose the right position. It's easier to cane accurately, at least if you're new to it, if the young lady is

lying down (perhaps on a bed with a pillow under her hips to lift her bottom up – the top can then stand to the side of the bed). If not, having you bend over something (a chair back, a desk if you have one) is easier than touching-your-toes.

4. Aim at the right spot. Be careful not to whack too high (watch out for the tail bone, particularly) or too low (the crease between the buttocks and thighs is usually seen as a sensible lowest point). Some tops mark the boundaries – the first stroke at the top of the "range", the second at the bottom, which then it makes it easier to land the remainder on target.

5. Don't hurry. Twenty seconds or so between strokes is good, to let the impact of the stroke reach its maximum point and level out, before applying the next one.

6. Don't "wrap". The worst marks come if the cane tip doesn't land on the buttocks, but goes right round onto the hips or front of the thighs. Making sure he doesn't stand too close will help.

7. Don't be tempted to whack too hard, or too many times, especially the first time. I know I was tempted to give my first spankee thirty of the best. Six, slowly, well-done with cuddles afterwards can be far more intense. And the cane doesn't need to hit the ceiling on the backswing! (Whilst getting used to wielding the cane, it may also be easier to hold it some way along, thus effectively shortening its length – that can help with accuracy until he's confident).

8. Close the windows, and put on the TV if you're at all worried about noise travelling. You want to enjoy it together – not have a worry at the back of your minds

about the neighbours hearing and calling the police to rescue the poor woman being beaten next door.

9. Have an appropriate safeword. Sounds obvious, but "no", "it hurts", "owwww" and "stoooopppppp" may well come out naturally – yet you may actually be enjoying it (deep down) and wanting the scene to continue. Traffic lights work well (amber = OMG it hurts, so be careful, but keep going; red = stop now).

10. Don't panic if the odd stroke does go astray. It may well do so – even with experienced players, the odd one does!

11. Have some arnica cream handy (if you can find some), or aloe vera if not, or decent moisturiser if not, and rub it in afterwards.

12. Don't book a session at the local spa, or in the local swimming pool with vanilla friends, for the following morning! You may have marks that might take a couple of days to fade!

And finally – have fun!

Afraid of the dark

By Abel on 22 April 2008

I stayed in a hotel in the deep Hampshire countryside last month: a lovely little rural pub converted into a very chic little restaurant-with-rooms. Everything was quite perfect – until a power cut at three in the morning, which caused something electronic to splutter a dying bleep, waking me with a start.

It was *dark*. Not your normal dark – dark backlit by the faint glow of city lights, of street lamps, of distant passing cars – but properly, I'm-in-the-middle-of-nowhere dark.

As I lay on the bed, unable to get back to sleep, I whiled away some of the time imagining a kinky variant of this pitch black world. The prison cells lined a narrow corridor, deep in some dank stone dungeon. No natural light here, just the flicker of the torches flaming on the walls. And before the guards departed for the evening, even those would be extinguished, leaving the women – the king's captured enemies? – engulfed by the absolute darkness until morning.

Except, some nights, their captors would return in the middle of the night. The prisoners would wake at the sound of the dungeon door being unbolted, at the stomp of approaching boots. Each girl would be praying: don't let it be my turn. The guards, carrying candles, would stop outside the designated cell; would open it; would enter and step through the crowd of occupants to unlock the chains of the girl who was to be taken and whipped.

Schoolgirl again

By Haron on 30 April 2008

I have a persistent dream in which I'm forced to return to school. It's the real me, at my real age, after getting my real degree. I get a letter that says I've been missing lessons, and unless I want my parents to be arrested, I should come to school.

Last night I had to sit a history test. (It was helpfully written in Latin.) The teacher kept lecturing me that, just because I'd spent ten years in higher education, I wasn't too special to obey the law and go to school.

I woke up from the nightmare paralysed with despair of failing the test, and tried to calm myself with how I wished the dream would have gone if I could have directed it.

Instead of taunting me, the teacher would have been sympathetic. Of course, it was hard to become a schoolgirl again, to obey the rules imposed by grown-ups when you've been a grown-up yourself for a while.

It was hard, but I still had to obey the law; to come to lessons when I was told, to do the homework, to keep my cheeky remarks to myself. He would help me as much as he could. But if he thought I was being obstinate...

Here he would pause significantly, and flick a look into the corner of the classroom, where one of my friends would be standing with her skirt up, her spanked bottom facing the class. "I won't enjoy doing it, but I will, if I think you need it. I will spank you, for your own good."

But the dream didn't go like that. Maybe next time. If I have to tread the dreamland as a schoolgirl again, I might at least have a spanking to make up for it.

The first girls' reformatory

By Abel on 5 May 2008

I've been reading about The Red Lodge, Britain's first reformatory for girls. The enlightened founder believed that the girls could be educated without regular recourse to corporal punishment. But I can imagine one resident pushing her luck too far: absconding for a third time, perhaps, having been given a very clear final warning.

She would be brought before the Governors. That, in itself, would cause her to quake: any bravado would have been long abandoned by the time she was led into the room. They would ask for an explanation; she would have none. They would warn her of the dire fate that might befall a homeless girl wandering the streets of Victorian Bristol. They would ask whether she recalled her previous warning:

"Yes, sir."

"Then we cannot allow this to go unpunished." They would confer amongst themselves, before the Chairman of the Governors turned back to her. "We intend to make an example of you, girl. We cannot allow the staff here to be undermined, and you were given very clear warnings."

"Please, sir. Have mercy…"

"You are to be birched at nine prompt tomorrow morning." The Chairman would turn to the warden: "Please make sure the girl is washed and put into a clean dress tomorrow morning, and bring her to the Oak Room at five to nine. Now take her away…"

—

A small group would gather in the Oak Room the following morning: the Chairman, with birch rods in hand. A governor or two. The warden of the reformatory. And the girl.

She'd be ordered to remove her dress, before being tied over the end of a long oak table. The Chairman would stand back: "I think we should wait until nine, gentlemen." And so they'd pause, listening for the bells of the neighbouring church. Counting each of the nine peals. Knowing that the other girls in the reformatory would also be counting, would also be holding their breath.

Pausing, once silence reigned.

And then beginning her thrashing: hard, measured, teaching a lesson that even the most tolerant of reformatories knows how to punish when punishment is due.

Spanked on the school trip

By Abel on 20 May 2008

I'm speaking at a conference in Palm Springs next week, and (as often happens before I have a major presentation to give) I find myself rewriting my speech in my sleep. New content comes and goes; pictures of the audience flash into life; I wake up and scribble down any bright ideas.

See, it's not just kinky stuff that fills my dreams. But last night the two merged. It was no longer a conference, but a school trip, and I was the master in charge. The group was sitting round a common room in the hostel we'd rented. (I imagine days spent walking up mountains in bracing fresh air, muddy boots left in the porch, steaming mugs of tea on our return). They were all good girls – the elite of the sixth-form; good friends.

Suddenly, the atmosphere changed. As an argument developed, one of the girls (my favourite, as it happened) raised not only her voice but her hand, slapping her adversary.

I intervened immediately, of course, before things got out of hand. She was sent from the room to wait for me outside my room; the remaining girls were lectured as to how disappointed I was in them. I made them tidy the room, wash up their mugs, and sent them early to bed.

She'd been waiting a fair while as a result before I made it to my room: her face was already tear-stained. I took her inside: her apologies were so heartfelt that scolding was barely necessary. But "you understand that I cannot let this go unpunished" made her nod, and "you realise how fighting would be dealt with were we at school" led to a murmured "I'd be caned, sir."

"Would you rather I informed your housemaster on our return, or dealt with this now?"

A pause, plucking up the courage. "Now, please, sir."

No canes here, on a school trip. I pulled up an armchair, and instructed her to lower her jeans and knickers to her ankles, and bend over my knees. The spanking was hard – very hard: if a girl was to take a caning-equivalent, then each smack had to count. She wriggled, cried, subsided. Stood afterwards, as I held her and told her that it was all over and there was nothing to worry about.

The poor, poor shower curtain!
By Abel on 24 May 2008

"I'm going to have a bath." So how could I resist? I waited until Haron was undressed and about to step into the deep, warm, bubbly water, and stormed in – cane in hand. "What on earth do you think you're playing at, young lady?"

She giggled, and tried to look serious. I thought I'd better explain. "Did I not tell you very clearly that you were to report to your housemaster straight after the game? And yet I find you've ignored me and come to get washed and changed."

She was trying hard not to smile, as she yes-sirred me.

"Now get into the bath, and stand with your hands on the wall."

"But it's hot...."

"Well more of you will be hot in a moment. This will teach you to get sent off playing hockey."

Six strokes followed: quite nasty little cutting ones. On the fourth, my backswing may have been at an odd angle: the trajectory of the cane made it catch a glancing blow on the shower curtain on its way down. She squeaked with surprise at the odd impact that resulted. "Quiet girl: that will have hurt the shower curtain far more than it hurt you."

Somehow we avoided collapsing into peals of laughter before the final two had been administered. And then I left her in peace, to sit down in the hot bath on her freshly-hot stripes.

A punishing schedule?

By Abel on 27 May 2008

I never can fathom the vagaries of airline security. Take your laptop out of your bag here; leave it encased there. Remove your shoes; pad barefoot through the grime. The only consistency is that they seem to think that humans have at least four hands, to hold all of the items which we've had to unpack or from which we've disrobed by the time we brave the scanners.

Our local airport seems particularly prone to making it up as they go along. As I headed out towards the States at the weekend, the young lady looked me up and down, and smiled ever-so-sweetly. Politely, she made her request: "Please remove your belt, sir."

I suddenly realised that I'd found many a girl's ideal job: eyeing up the toppish looking men, and getting that certain frisson as she watched them whip out their belts.

I folded mine neatly, doubling it over carefully before placing it on top of the tray before her. I smiled. She smiled back. I wondered...

One in ten

By Abel on 31 May 2008

The headmaster was evidently furious, as he lectured the hastily-assembled sixth-formers from the stage. "In all of my years as a schoolmaster, I have never encountered such wilful misconduct by such a large group of girls."

"I am minded to give each and every one of you six of the best." Stunned silence: girls winced, threw scared glances at their friends, reached for neighbours' hands.

He paused, as if for effect. "But I fear that the time involved in punishing so many of you would prove unacceptably disruptive to the school day, and so I intend to adapt the Roman approach to quelling insubordination in the ranks. I shall therefore select one girl in every ten at random; each of those chosen will find a letter in their pigeonhole before chapel tomorrow morning, asking them to report to my study before lunch to be caned."

—

Amazing the kinky concepts one dreams up with ten hours to kill on a transatlantic flight. No idea what they'd done – mass truancy, a brawl with a neighbouring school, boycotting a session with an eminent visiting speaker? But I rather enjoyed the idea, even if it's entirely impractical for a play scene – after all, the nine girls left out would be distraught!

Naughty girls on the news

By Haron on 1 June 2008

Last night was the final night when it was allowed to drink on the London Underground. According to the BBC, a great mob showed up at Liverpool Street Station yesterday to party to the last day of drinking away – a big enough crowd that they had to shut the station.

Oh, dear. What a pair of the partying girls didn't realise was that their father would watch the news, just as the event was being reported, and would spot two familiar laughing faces, two heads of curly blonde hair, their hands clutched around bottles of beer.

When they returned home – on the bus, because they'd stopped the Tube, how cool! – he would be waiting for them in the hallway, hands folded on his chest. And as soon as they saw his face, their giggly smiles would melt away – they would know that he knew.

He wouldn't spank his girls just then: who knew how much beer they'd drunk. He would want them sober, alert and contrite. He would dispatch them to their bedrooms at once, and inform them they were grounded for the whole of the following week. And that he would deal with them in the morning.

In fact, he might be punishing them right now: one girl in the corner of the living room with her hands on her head, the other – over daddy's lap, kicking and squealing as the smooth-backed hairbrush descends.

The alarmed call

By Abel on 6 June 2008

"Good morning, sir. This is your six a.m. wake-up call."

I was just awake enough to reply: "But I booked the call for eight o'clock."

Pause. "Oh." Pause. "I'm sorry, sir, I think I've just misread the handwriting on our list. I'm really sorry."

The solution seemed obvious to me. After all, I had a paddle and cane in my suitcase.

It took a few moments for her to arrive at my door – flustered, contrite. She noticed the implements on the table as soon as she entered; looked at me in momentary panic.

"It seems, young lady, that you need to be taught the difference between six and eight."

"Yes, sir."

"Remove your skirt and come and stand in the middle of the room with your hands on your head."

She folded her uniform neatly over the back of the chair; adopted the pose. I circled around her. "Why so careless?"

"It was a mistake, sir. Really: I've never done it before."

I pulled down her knickers; let them drop to her ankles. Still circled: "And what happens to girls who make mistakes?"

"They get punished, sir."

"Then you shall bend over the back of the armchair, and take the consequences of your carelessness. I shall start with six swats of the paddle. And I'll finish with eight strokes of the cane..."

* At some point this account and reality diverge somewhat!

Looking at their hands
By Haron on 14 June 2008

In my dream, I was a princess, a king's younger sister. I had been promised to somebody since I was young, but some sort of political trouble recently made my hand available again, and ambassadors have started to swarm around the palace.

I knew I would never be allowed to marry for love, but my brother promises to listen to my preferences as far as possible. Portraits of dukes and princes are delivered to me, and I walk around the makeshift gallery of possible husbands. I look at their faces, sure, but most of all I look at their hands.

Which one looks strong? Which lap would I most like to tumble over? Which one of them looks like I could push him just far enough, but not further, before he grasps me by the upper arm and draws me to his rooms for a spanking?

I guess, if I were a princess, I'd be a little bit shallow.

Back to face her first caning

By Abel on 22 June 2008

My darling wife's due home before very long: she's been acting as a Florence Nightingale looking after her parents, and I can't wait to hold and hug her. Oh, and to spank her, of course.

I've been toying with ideas for the "first scene back". Much as I want to up-end her over my knee for an OTK hand-spanking, it seems a shame to waste the comparatively rare opportunity of her having a bottom that's gone unwhacked for quite so long.

So I'm picturing a schoolgirl, in a renowned college where corporal punishment is very much the last resort. housemasters and housemistresses can and do cane, but it's a comparatively occasional occurrence. And those rare canings are more ceremonial than cruel: it's the very act of bending over to be caned (a maximum of four strokes, across a girl's skirt, with a light cane) that punishes more than the pain.

It's the headmasterial canings that are truly to be dreaded. He always gives six strokes. Always on the bare. Always with a senior cane. But only one, maybe two girls per term find their way to his study. And Haron could be one of them...

Or it's the end of term. The three sisters know the tradition: they line up outside Daddy's study on the first evening home, and one-by-one are called in to hand him their school report. They watch as he reads, crave his praise, dread his disapproval. He reads nice comments aloud: "I'm so pleased with Mrs Watson's comments about your hard work in Geography this term." And he raises an eyebrow, and asks for an explanation of any misconduct or shortcomings.

The end of every discussion is marked with a hug, and a "lovely to have you home". Only on some occasions, where a girl has fallen short of the high standards that she and he would expect, that hug is prefaced by an instruction to "take down the cane from the top of the bookcase", and a carefully-administered, loving correction.

Haron's always been the good girl of the three: the one who comes top of her class, who shines even more than her ever-so-clever sisters. She's listened over the years as the two elder girls have gone in before her. She's learned to worry for them if the conversation has started to drag on for much longer than usual. She's heard the whacks, the sobs; participated in the cuddles afterwards. And, as the youngest, she's then gone in last – to be praised. Always, to be praised.

This time it's different: the first year she's been alone in the line, her sisters now at University. And it's the first time she's known that the report she's held in her trembling hands would disappoint, her lack of self-discipline in the run-up to the exams reflected in a series of unacceptably low marks...

150 of the best

By Abel on 24 June 2008

There are those in the scene who struggle to take six of the best; there are others who are disappointed if the tally comes to less than sixty. One of the tests of a good top is therefore their ability to tailor the scene and the whacking to the preferences of their play partner. Give the "six" girl sixty, and she'd rightly scream blue murder.

Give the "sixty" girl six, and she'd wonder why a light tickling was now classed as a thrashing.

Our friend Cath falls into the latter category: only a really hard, sustained series of strokes will do. One evening earlier in the month, she and I played a scene in which I gave her fifty with a new, particularly mean cane, and she took it remarkably bravely. (Until stroke forty-two, hey, Cath?).

Cuddling afterwards, and admiring her stripes, my Machiavellian side came to the fore. "So, young lady: that concludes the first part of your sentence."

See, when the courts sentenced a girl to 150 strokes, the prison's punishment officer would only give her 50 on the first evening. That'd be enough to punish the girl severely, to make her realise how painful a flogging could be – and to spend the night dreading the remaining 100 (twice as many again! over existing marks!) to be administered the following morning. Thus, rather than one painful whacking, over in minutes, the ordeal would be drawn out over hours.

We concluded that she'd been caught tearing down The Party's propaganda, replacing it with her own subversive posters. Her thrashing would serve both to punish her, and to make an example of her to others who may have contemplated undermining the authority of their government.

The pained look on Cath's face every time she sat down the following day was delightful to behold – even if each wince quickly gave way to a big grin! I, on the other hand, seemed to develop a mild form of Repetitive Strain Injury from the experience, the pain in my right wrist for days after making typing at work remarkably painful.

The spanking amnesty

By Haron on 26 June 2008

To celebrate my homecoming after the ridiculously long time apart, Abel took a day off.

It's June, and we're in London, so it would have been wrong not to go shopping in the sales – so we did. We rode a long escalator in Debenhams, with enormous red "50% off" signs flapping around us like flags.

We imagined a similar sign outside a headmaster's door at the end of the term. "50% off your punishment." The Head would announce at assembly that he still had some offences from the previous term, where the culprits were unknown. He really wanted to deal with the events, and not allow them to drag on until the following term, and so he would offer an amnesty.

Any culprit who came to his office and admitted to any misdeeds before the end of term, would receive half the usual number of strokes.

If, however, she didn't come forward, but was somehow discovered during the following term, she would receive the full punishment, plus an extra 50% for her cowardice.

I can imagine girls who'd committed relatively minor offences being quite torn. The chances of being discovered for something small weren't great, particularly after a long time – but if they didn't come forward, a relatively light punishment would suddenly expand by half.

I'm not actually sure what I'd do under the circumstances...

A welcome home whipping

By Haron on 28 June 2008

After my return from a month's exile, it didn't take Abel too long to remind me that life isn't all shopping trips and drinks in the pub. No sooner than we made it back from the airport and had some food, he innocently said:

"Do you like my new belt?"

I looked. And closed my eyes, to see if the monstrosity would go away if I blinked. And then I looked again. The belt was still there: the thickest, widest strip of leather I've ever seen, liberally decorated with massive metal studs. With a belt like that, Abel would have been welcome at a hard rock festival. He was clearly delighted at having sneaked in a purchase like that while I wasn't looking.

I honestly told him that the belt suited him very much. And that I was sure it was purely decorative.

For a short while I even believed it to be so. He sat on the bed and invited me over his lap, and he reminded me what a spanking felt like. (A note, in case I ever actually forget: at first it feels kind of warm and lovely, and then he gets into the swing of things, at which point it hurts like hell and you begin to wonder what you're doing in the same room as this monster, never mind being married to him.)

After my bottom felt like I had accidentally sat on a bee hive, Abel sternly ordered me to bend over the bed. I cautiously looked around the room, wondering whether he'd brought anything from home to use on me, and saw to my dismay that he'd picked up the monster belt.

He considerately folded it the soft side out, with the metal bits safely covered up, and asked me how many strokes I thought were appropriate for the occasion. I bit my tongue on "none," and suggested six. And you know what? Even folded – and even used quite lightly – that belt is a good candidate for a charity give-away some time when Abel isn't looking. I did get one really hard stroke – the final one, aimed across the tops of my thighs – and it made me question whether I was still into spanking at all.

Five minutes later, however, the sharp pain turned into a comfortable glow, the smacks turned into hugs, and I knew I was home again.

A sadistic vacation

By Abel on 29 June 2008

According to a report earlier this month in The Guardian, Pierre Cardin is spending millions in an attempt to turn the small town of Lacoste into a cultural enclave. The place has an interesting history:

Only the imposing, half-ruined castle that once belonged to the Marquis de Sade hints as a darker truth of the feudal rulers who lorded it over the villagers in this south-eastern corner of France... de Sade's chateau [is] said to have inspired the gothic settings for his novels of sexual perversion.

Cardin has "spent millions restoring the castle" and his plans for the village include "luxury hotels, a top restaurant, a de Sade café and a piano bar."

A *de Sade café*?!! The mind just boggles. I suspect that the conditions of employment for the waitresses are likely to be rather strict. And is it too much to hope that one of said hotels might be located in the castle itself, all themed rooms, whips available from room service and "would sir care to make use of the dungeon"?

The Punishment Committee

By Haron on 7 July 2008

Over the weekend we visited our favourite private library, which provides us with so much inspiration and material for our historical posts. We captured a strategically placed table, stacked it with promising-looking volumes and set to research.

On the other end of the reading room, the library regulars were convening over their newspapers, coffee and biscuits.*

"That's the punishment committee," Abel murmured in my ear. "They are having their weekly meeting."

I looked at the tweed jackets and home-knitted cardigans, the tidy hair, the sombre expressions, the tobacco stains on the fingers of the older men, and realised that Abel was right. This *had* to be the local punishment committee.

As well as receiving parents who came here with their grievances, these conscientious members of the community would go through the local papers, looking for reports of misbehaviour by the young people.

They would discuss each instance in a polite debate, decide on the most appropriate measures. The secretary would write up a notice for the culprit, who would have a week to submit any defences or objections.

These would be looked at – and most certainly dismissed – at the following meeting, after which a volunteer from among the committee members would be dispatched to the culprit's house armed with punishment instructions and a suitable implement. Case closed.

It's amazing how innocent these people looked in the bright light of Saturday morning, while accomplishing such tasks in plain view of the reading public.

* You're allowed to talk and eat in this room. In fact, they

sell you the food. I nearly had a heart attack the first time I saw somebody munch a lemon drizzle cake over a 19th-century book, but I guess they trust you to be careful.

Best maid in show
By Haron on 9 July 2008

The Great Yorkshire Show is in full swing today, with all the flowers, cattle and local crafts shown off on its huge grounds.

I wonder if in years past it was customary for the great houses to enter the competition for the best maid.

The girls in their tidiest, cleanest uniforms would stand in a line on a raised stage. The judges would call up each of them by turn to ask a few questions. The winner would be determined in a secret, heated debate. Most maids would consider it an honour to be entered into the County Show, but there would, of course, be an odd sullen girl, who would have to be threatened with a switch by the housekeeper, before she could be pushed onto the stage.

"What do you like about working in Ravenwood Hall?" one judge would ask.

She would glower at him: "What would you like about getting up before the crack of dawn, fetching and carrying all day, and being slapped around by an old witch?"

(Somewhere in the crowd, the housekeeper all but explodes with rage.)

It isn't just a switching that's in store for her now, but a sound birching at the hands of the butler, with all of the servants present, and the master himself supervising the event.

The house in Vienna
By Abel on 11 July 2008

We're going on holiday to Austria in a few weeks' time. I can't wait. But we have one slight problem: we're travelling in a small group – with the "would overhear any activity in the neighbouring room in the suite" type of fellow travellers. So I can tell now that Haron's not going to get spanked all week.

It's made me daydream. Some grand old Viennese house: tall, imposing, high ceilings, ornate. Very Habsburg.

Haron, despatched on her own at the agreed time, "to meet one of her distant relatives who lives in the city". ("No, it's OK. I won't go with her. I don't speak the language." Excuses, excuses, to cover the real reason for her trip).

She's smartly dressed. She checks the address carefully, knocks on the door. A young woman opens, all blonde and neat, in a crisp uniform. "Miss Haron? You are expected."

She is shown along a corridor, to a closed door. The maid leaves her: "You should knock at the door, and wait until Herr Professor calls you."

She knocks. He makes her wait.

Minutes later, a strongly-accented voice. "You may enter."

He makes Haron stand before his desk. Looks at her, over his glasses, studying her intently as if trying to read her mind. Peers down, picks up a letter from his desk, reads it carefully. "Your husband informs me that your behaviour here in our city has been most disappointing. He has sent you to me to be punished. You understand that?"

A quiet confirmation.

"I can't hear you, young lady."

"Yes, sir." Louder, voice still trembling.

The gentleman stands, reaches up to the bookcase. The implement he takes down comprises three long, straight, thick switches, tied together at one end. "I had my maid make this freshly this morning. Now undress."

As Haron strips, shyly, for punishment, he rings a bell; the maid re-appears, almost instantaneously. (Later, he will question her; will find that she was listening at the door; will birch her).

"Miss Haron, please bend over the end of my desk. Liesel, please go to the opposite side of the desk, and hold Miss Haron's hands, firmly. She is not to move during her punishment."

And so the gentleman whips my wife, her cries quite lost between the thick walls of the mansion, as Liesel pins her tightly in position.

Haron dresses afterwards. Thanks the gentleman through her tears. And then the maid shows her out into the bright Viennese sunshine.

Wasting police time
By Abel on 12 July 2008

I did feel just a tad sorry for the girl I dreamt of the other night. She was standing before the Chief of Police in his office; he was lecturing her sternly. "Quite fair and reasonable punishment... A mischievous complaint, totally without foundation in law..."

Earlier in the day, it seemed, she'd presented herself at the local police station to complain. She lived in the big house, she explained (a daughter, a ward, a maid?) and had been soundly whipped that morning for some misdemeanour. "And it's not fair, and it wasn't my fault, and they shouldn't have the right to do it."

The constable had taken her into a cell and made her show her marks: six fresh stripes, vivid, neatly and expertly laid-on. And then he'd taken a statement, and recorded the details, and summoned the butler from the House to give evidence. ("Yes, officer, all of the girls in the house are well aware that misconduct will result in a thrashing"). Forms had been filled in, a report filed.

The Chief was most unimpressed. "Wasting police time – a most serious offence," he continued, explaining that they had mentioned the situation to his Lordship, who was in complete agreement with the proposed course of action.

"Constable?"

Snapping to attention: "Sir?"

The Chief looked from him to the girl, and back again. "Strip her and tie her over the back of the chair, then fetch me a birch…"

Their post-punishment apologies

By Abel on 24 July 2008

The herd of baby elephants in the hotel room directly above mine had been practising their gymnastics for far too long, far too late at night. Reluctantly, I picked up the phone to the reception desk, to ask whether they might be able to ask my fellow guests to quieten down.

Silence descended within moments, and I was able to fall asleep at last.

To sleep, perchance to dream… Two girls in the room: best friends, on a trip to London. The father of one, staying further down the corridor, oblivious to the post-lights-out misbehaviour. The hotel manager, knocking on his door to mention the problem, accompanying him to the girls' room to order them to quieten down.

The door shutting behind the manager, the girls' apologies too late to save them. They'd be told to bend over the ends of their twin beds, to lower their pyjama bottoms. He'd whip his own daughter first – she'd be used to the taste of his belt. And then to her friend, who'd agree quietly that her own parents had told her that she should behave impeccably during the trip, and that they had asked her friend's father to punish her soundly if she did not. The same dozen strokes, the same tears.

And the same order at the end of their punishment: to put on their dressing gowns and go downstairs to apologise to the gentlemen below for the disturbance they'd caused; to explain that they had been dealt with; to promise that there'd be no repetition.

Vienna calling
By Abel on 30 July 2008

We've been doing the touristy thing all week. Forget the grand Habsburg buildings and great museums: the baby panda in the zoo rates as the highlight so far.

Food here's interesting. We stumbled into the hotel's restaurant on the first night in jeans and T-shirts, sat outside on the terrace, ordered beers – and then discovered that the chef who created the menu has two Michelin stars! The following evening took us to a more traditional place, recommended by a business acquaintance of mine who lives in the city.

Figlmüller has been serving Viennese specialities since 1905. It's an old-fashioned, serious place: the staff are professional, but somewhat formal and scary. The queues outside are daunting – we were lucky, getting in within a mere half-hour's wait.

As we arrived, a cute young American woman and her mother were finishing their food at the next table. The daughter turned to a passing waiter and asked for the cheque. A few moments later, he reappeared at our table with the menus and she leant over to ask again – a little irritably.

"But of course, madam," he replied, reaching into his pocket and taking out the bill that he'd been away preparing.

I rather thought he should have kept the slip in his pocket. "Indeed, young lady. Would you care to follow me to the cashier's office?"

Through a back door, into a dark room. "Now, perhaps you would care to explain why you felt it necessary to be so rude?"

She would apologise, beg their forgiveness.

The strap hanging on the wall would have been used countless times over the past century. He'd take it down, flex it. "You see, young lady, we take a traditional view here. As you're about to learn."

She'd protest, but he'd be stronger than her: she'd quickly find herself tossed over his knee, skirt lifted for a thrashing...

...and then he'd allow her to pay the bill.

Back in reality, somewhat later – whilst we ate our much-renowned Schnitzels – we became aware of a slight kerfuffle at the door. A young lady had pushed to the front of the queue: "We made a reservation for 8pm."

The maitre d' checked his lists. Arched eyebrows: "Did you?"

She fell silent, then shame-facedly confessed that she had not. He sent the blushing girl scurrying away, her tail between her legs. Only I rather wished that he'd invited her in: shown her too through to that back room, taken down the strap again before revealing that he knew she was being dishonest, and giving her the choice: "I can either call the police and report you for deception, or you can bend over the chair and we will deal with this here and now."

Abel is naughty
By Haron on 31 July 2008

When we came back to our hotel room last night, and picked up the "do not disturb" sign to put on our door, Abel got an evil glint in his eye.
"I could do something very bad," he said. "Shall I?"
"What is it?"
He waved the second sign at me, the "please clean my room" one. Then he tiptoed across the hotel corridor and hung it on the door of the room opposite, where the inhabitants were, presumably, peacefully asleep.
In fairness, he took it off right away. But the naughtiness, the naughtiness! What would have happened to me if I'd so much as suggested it?
In the fine tradition of the spanking blogs everywhere, I'd like to take some suggestions on what punishment Abel deserves.
(No, he's not going to accept it. Ah, well, we can dream.)

The Imperial silverware
By Abel on 1 August 2008

The Imperial Silverware display in Vienna's Hofburg palace leads straight onto the tour of the emperor's apartments. Was it any wonder that I immediately connected the two?
The Emperor looked up from the dinner table, visibly irritated. "There appears to be some commotion," he observed to his head butler, who was hovering – as usual – in the shadows.

"I believe, Your Majesty, that one of the serving girls has just been caught trying to steal a piece of the silverware that she was clearing from the banquet."

"Then they'd better bring her in, so that we may see her punished. I presume you will deal with her for me?"

"I have already sent to the Riding School for a whip, Your Majesty."

The girl was dragged into the room, and bent over a chair. The assembled gentlemen turned to watch, as the butler took up the crop. She squealed as he started to lay on the whipping – wriggling as if to get away, staying in position mindful of the further thrashing she would doubtless receive if she did. Six strokes marked their way across her skirt, before the butler told her to stand.

A deep voice boomed across the room – the emperor: "And when, pray, are you going to start punishing her *properly?*" There was a pause, a confused silence, before he continued. "The girls who work here need to understand the severity of stealing from the imperial family."

"Yes, Your Majesty. Would you like me to continue her thrashing?"

The emperor looked at the girl, as if weighing the conflicting courses of discipline and mercy. "No, I don't think I would."

But if the girl looked relieved, it was only for a moment, as he continued: "You shall take her to my chambers and I will whip her personally. Strip her, wash her, and have her tied tightly over my desk. And send a footman out into the gardens; have him cut six switches from one of the birch trees, and tie them firmly together. I intend to make something of an example out of young... what was your name?"

"Charlotte, sir."

"Yes, Charlotte." The emperor looked around the table. "I really must apologise for this most unfortunate incident." He clapped his hands: "Well, what are you waiting for? Take her away and prepare her to be punished. And meanwhile: pour us some more wine – my guests are dying of thirst."

The punished princess
By Haron on 4 August 2008

Elisabeth of Bavaria was only fifteen years old when, accompanied by her stern mother, she was dispatched to Vienna to marry the Emperor of Austria, Franz Joseph.

She entered the city in the Imperial Carriage, the awesome structure with wheels taller than an average human. The carriage in question is now part of the collection in the Schönbrunn Palace. The accompanying display tells the story of how the young princess got into some difficulty trying to exit the carriage: she knocked her crown on the top of the door.

She saw this as a bad omen and burst into tears, and thus arrived into her new home sobbing her heart out.

I suspect she was also crying because she knew: as soon as she was installed into her apartments, her mother would seek her out, carrying the ebony hairbrush, with which the princesses of Bavaria were so familiar.

In a few days Elisabeth would become the Empress Consort, but for now she was still in her mother's power, and her display in front of the gawking commoners had been disgraceful. Bent over her mother's lap, the princess would be spanked soundly and mercilessly, for what she hoped would be the last time in her life.

Interestingly, later in life Elisabeth was responsible for abolishing corporal punishment in the Austrian army. Compassion can be a great tool for rulers. Perhaps, her mother had thought about this too.

The flea-market hunt

By Haron on 8 August 2008

Our Viennese guidebook informed us that, just a few minutes' walk from our hotel, we could find the site of a major weekly flea-market.

Abel immediately lit up with the idea of finding a pile of implements discarded by retired Austrian disciplinarians, parents of teenagers who'd left for university, and other folks who may not need their collections any more.

Although we didn't discover a great deal of spanking paraphernalia amidst the mountains of delightfully insane stuff the locals were selling off that day, we were not disappointed on our quest. We came across a weaver's stand, and were immediately drawn to his vast display of carpet-beaters in all sorts of sizes and designs.

The one we picked up was a perfect specimen: of a medium size, so that it can cover but not dwarf a naughty girl's bottom, nicely woven, but not too paddle-like in density; all the knots in the rattan were polished away, all the joints sanded smooth. It came back with us, and waited for its hour.

This didn't come until we were installed in our hotel back in Heathrow, free of our delightful, but limiting vanilla company. Abel rummaged in the suitcase and emerged with the carpet-beater at the ready.

I was suddenly not sure I liked it any more.

"What, now?"

"Yes, now, young lady. Over the bed. Quickly now, I need to re-pack."

This last made us both giggle. Ah, the romance of a relationship in its seventh year! I assumed the position with no more protestations.

The delicate-looking toy cracked into my skin with a vicious bite. I belatedly remembered its original purpose.

No wonder it hurt; carpets world over would quiver before its wrath.

"Ouch!" I complained when it struck again. "That's nasty!" I attempted to stand up, but Abel lightly pushed me in the back.

"Stay down," he said sternly. "You didn't think you would get away with any less than six of the best?"

My argument was going to be that, although made of rattan, this was hardly a cane, so traditional numbers of strokes didn't apply, but I had no time to express this complex objection. Abel took a swing and gave me a great whack, which he followed with three more in quick succession. I wailed, jumped up and clutched my bottom. The sensation was not unlike it must be to be caned with five canes at once.

"I think this works," said Abel smugly. Hmm, yes, I think so.

The carpet-beater was zipped away into the suitcase, and our Austrian adventure was truly over. However, writing this on the train home, I can feel a ghost of sting as I shift in my seat. As far as holiday mementos go, this one is proving quite lasting.

Another girl's punishment

By Haron on 12 August 2008

Taking notes at a leather-topped desk in the library, I noticed that indentations from the pressure of the pen stayed on the leather for a while after you were finished.

I imagined watching a girl at another desk work hard all morning, scribbling away on her notepaper, hardly noticing anything around. When she finished her work, she would sigh with relief, lean back in her chair and check what she'd written, while absent-mindedly massaging her wrist. Then she would glance at her watch, hurriedly gather her paper and leave.

I would move to her desk, because it's better lit, with a more comfortable chair. And only as I start laying out my own notes, would I notice the traces in the leather, the ghost of that other girl's work.

She hasn't been taking notes: she was writing lines: "I will always complete my assignments on time and to the best of my ability. I will always complete my assignments on time and to the best of my ability." Hundreds of lines, judging by the time she has taken over them.

I would cross my fingers on her behalf, that she hands the lines in on time, and that they are neat enough to satisfy her tutor. I have a fair idea of what would happen if he were displeased.

The Park Plaza perverts

By Abel on 13 August 2008

We spent a night recently – before setting out on our Viennese trip – in the lovely Park Plaza hotel, near County Hall in London. Great location, great suite – shame they can't mix a decent cocktail.

My inner trainspotter (very inner!) was delighted to find our room had a marvellous view over Waterloo station: our own private train set to watch from on high through floor-to-ceiling windows.

My not-all-inner trainspotter was equally delighted. Haron and Cath were called into the station master's office. He scolded them for being caught without tickets, pointed out all of the decent, honest folks down on the platforms below who'd doubtless paid their fares.

Stripped, the girls were made to bend forward with their hands on the windows. Told to watch the station as they took their punishment. Six strokes each with the cane followed, with much squealing (especially, it must be said, from Haron).

And then I took up my trusty Lochgelly: "The caning was for the return journey to Waterloo, on which you were caught. Yet you can't have had tickets for the outward journey either." Six each with the tawse followed. Much squealing again. From them both, this time.

They looked sorry for themselves, it must be said. Even sorrier when I asked, "And which of you had the idea to evade your fares this morning?" Cath, bravely, owned up: six more of the XH seared home. And then we could cuddle.

Now, there's an interesting footnote to the scene, for I had to leave the girls in the room shortly afterwards to catch a train from the station down below. As I wandered along the platform, I noticed that the darkened glass in the windows didn't seem quite so darkened as we'd maybe imagined. I texted Haron: "I'm on the platform. Come to the window and wave."

Two cheerful young ladies appeared moments later: stark naked, waving enthusiastically. Clearly visible to anyone looking up. As indeed they must have been whilst being thrashed a half hour or so earlier. I am so glad to have offered such a salutary lesson in the penalties for fare dodging not only to my two girls, but to that morning's entire customer base of South West Trains.

The mafia punishment

By Abel on 15 August 2008

A high-ceilinged barn, in the middle of nowhere. Straw on the floor. Dark outside, bright artificial light illuminating the gathering inside. No risk of the group being disturbed as they meted out the punishment.

The girl had just been brought in, her eyes widening as her blindfold had been taken off and she'd recognised her captors. Six men, eight maybe? Hardened types, each holding an implement – a crop here, switches there, a doubled belt over there.

She was grasped roughly from behind, her clothes half unbuttoned, half ripped from her body before she was thrust forward over the table, tied in position.

I spoke to my comrades – like me, senior figures in the local mafia. Expressed my disappointment at her behaviour, which had led to one of our brothers being caught and imprisoned. Hoped that they would not hold back in teaching her a lesson. Invited the first of them forward.

We took turns. Whipped her until she begged for mercy, and offered her none. Waited my turn, before administering her final thrashing: slow, calculating, hard.

And then took turns to punish her some more. Intimately, in ways that I couldn't possible write about for fear of corrupting our more innocent readers...

Sometimes my dreams surprise me...

Thrashed before the Upper Ten

By Abel on 18 August 2008

I've been reading a truly fascinating history of Wentworth, the largest of the English country houses. (When I spotted it on the bookshelves in the ever-so-posh new Terminal 5 at Heathrow the other day, I was interested purely in learning more of English history: that a book on the lives of the governing classes and their staff might have kinky potential wasn't at all a factor in my purchasing decision. Honest!). The most interesting section comes when they discuss the dining arrangements:

Dinner in the Steward's Room had been as formal an affair as the one that was about to take place upstairs. "There were six separate dining halls for the servants, depending on your place in the hierarchy," recalled the son of the manager of the Wentworth estates. "The Steward's Room was the top dining room, reserved for the Upper Ten. It was terribly smart. They sat on Chippendale chairs."

The Upper Ten were the most senior servants in the hierarchy. They include the groom of the chambers, the housekeeper, the house steward, the butler, the under-butler, the head housemaid and the valets. They dined in style: a footman served them at a table laid with fine china and glass; the men wore smoking jackets or evening dress, the women, long silk gowns. Precedence was strictly observed.

As dinner concluded, coffee was served, followed by the usual digestifs – the senior staff enjoyed the same choice of port and liqueurs as their lordships downstairs. And then came the moment that certain of their more junior colleagues had been dreading all evening.

For a maid to misbehave in one of the great country houses was a serious offence, punishable with the utmost severity. For her to misbehave whilst accompanying her master on a visit to one of his peers was a matter of the utmost shame.

A bell would be rung; any girls who had fallen short of the highest standards, had let down their household, would enter the room. A nervous line-up, each girl wringing her hands, shifting from foot to foot, avoiding the eyes of her seniors. Her offence would be read out, discussed around the table, and the presiding servant would pronounce her sentence.

The punishment would vary according to the customs of the house in which they were staying. In some, she might find herself over the steward's knee for the hardest of hand-spankings. In others, a strap might be fetched, whilst in others a more junior servant would be sent to the stables to procure a riding crop from the grooms. The cane was the most common instrument of discipline, of course – with the birch reserved for the most serious offences. One servant, Mabel Ross, recalls its terrors: "They had the dining table cleared, and used rope to tie me in position. And then Lord Scarborough's butler lifted my skirt, and parted my underwear, and laid such a thrashing on me as I will never forget. I was a good girl after that, I swear: one birching is one too many for any girl."

—

OK, I confess. I rather digressed from the original text part way through. But one can use one's imagination, surely?

Kitchen pervertibles

By Haron on 24 August 2008

I should know better by now. I should know that when Abel says, "I need to go into a kitchen shop to replace XYZ," he actually means "I want to go into the wooden spoon section, to get something to beat you with." (OK, he probably wants to buy stuff to cook with too, but that motivation is definitely secondary.)

But yesterday I naively followed him into the shop, and stood by as he sorted through measuring jugs and other gizmos, only to see him pick up the thickest, scariest wooden spoon in the world. (Maybe it only seemed that way at the point, of course. The spoon you're about to get smacked with is always the worst ever.) Protestations were no use: it was clear that the thing was coming home with us.

I'd forgotten all about it by the time I ran my bath this morning, – only to get a nasty surprise when Abel walked into the bathroom, spoon in hand.

"Hands on the edge of the bath," he said snappily. The bubbles in the tub winked at me as I complied, promising me comfort after it was all over.

As the spoon swung back, I squeaked and twisted out of the way before it came anywhere near me.

"Hey, no moving!" Abel sounded surprised. "You get an extra one for that! I was going to give you four, but it's five now."

Now he tells me, I thought. He raised the spoon again, and this time I closed my eyes to keep from seeing it take aim. The swats were quick, crisp and agonising. I couldn't even tell how many I'd had, by the time it was over.

"Now get into the bath and sit," said Abel, watching smugly as I writhed around.

Good old kitchen shops. How I don't love them, let me count the ways.

Spanking roulette

By Haron on 31 August 2008

In my dream I was sentenced to corporal punishment. Not sure by whom, or for what misdeeds, but I was. I may have even deserved it.

The detail that turned the dream into a bona fide nightmare was that the implement and the number of strokes were to be decided by gambling.

I was handed a little hemp sack with something clinking inside. These were, I was told, pieces of ivory carved with symbols of implements. I had to put my hand into the sack and draw one. Once the implement was established, I would be handed a platter with ten-sided dice, which I would roll for the number of strokes.

I can still hear the sounds, ominous in the otherwise silent room: the ivory clicking, the dice rattling around the silver platter.

I'm not sure what the result was. I'm quite happy not to know, actually...

The floggings awaiting captured girls

By Abel on 4 September 2008

A most unusual dream last night. In it, Haron and one of our friends were both maidens in mediaeval times. An army was forming; the girls of the village were being pressed into service as archers.

They'd heard the rumours, though – that if the enemy caught any of the archers, they dealt out severe punishment. A captured girl could expect to be led to a nearby tree, her hands tied above her head with a rope suspended from a stout branch. The soldiers would tear open the back of her dress, then whip her soundly.

Needless to say, Haron and our friend were trying to escape their military duties. And, inevitably, I was insisting that they played their part for king and country.

(I think I may have watched too much of the archery when the Olympics was on!)

The implement suitcase

By Haron on 6 September 2008

Abel and I were walking up to the train station. He valiantly carried the suitcase, almost not complaining at all. Seriously, he only complained once.

"I can't believe how heavy it is!" he said.

"What have you got in there?" I asked, knowing that we were only going away for a couple of nights, so hardly needed any clothes.

"A strap, a cane, a tawse and a hairbrush," he said. And paused. And said: "Oh."

Right, he was only carrying a mini dungeon in that bag...

Court Circular

By Abel on 8 September 2008

It always astonishes me that, in 21st century Britain, the 'Court Circular' still appears in certain daily newspapers. The formal announcement describes the previous day's royal appointments – for example:

> Clarence House
>
> 20th August
>
> The Duchess of Rothesay, President, this afternoon attended the Brooke Hospital for Animals Garden Party in Aboyne and was received by Her Majesty's Lord-Lieutenant of Aberdeenshire (Mr Angus Farquharson).

Still, it could sometimes prove interesting:

> Buckingham Palace
>
> 1 September
>
> Princess Victoria this afternoon attended the Central London Women's Disciplinary Centre and was received by the Chief Punishment Officer (Sgt Jock McPherson).

Oh, how the papers would speculate – with paparazzi photos showing the tear-stained young royal appearing considerably more dishevelled on her way out from her appointment than she had been on the way in...

The mysterious punishment

By Haron on 9 September 2008

Last time we were in the wonderful private library of which we're members, Abel set off to look for a particular book in the catalogue. On the table next to the catalogue was a convenient desk for noting down the references, with some scraps of paper to save you writing on the back of your hand.

When he brought back the book, we noticed that the scrap paper once used to be some sort of a circular, a report from a meeting or something similar. It had half-phrases clipped off mid-word, but still making sense.

I imagined picking up one of these innocent-looking scraps to find something along the lines of:

> "Unfortunately, all warnings have proved ineffectu... required to administer six-of-the-best with a senio... have received the necessary consent form from M... witnesses."

It would have taken some pain-staking work to recreate the full circular, but I'm sure I wouldn't have been able to resist.

Maids in a country house

By Haron on 11 September 2008

Loathe to waste a weekend even when the weather is foul, we took ourselves for a day trip to a neighbouring National Trust country house, the beautiful Cragside. Even to a somewhat jaded country house visitor like yours truly ("What? Another historical kitchen with historical copper pots? Yawn!") Cragside offered enough unusual and quirky details to set my imagination going.

For one thing, being a relatively new house, belonging to a family that made its fortune in local industry, it had some technical features that rarely belong in my Victorian spanking fantasies.

There was, for example, a lift: it would take a maid from the cellar/scullery, via the kitchen, to the upstairs corridors. It had been specifically installed to ease the maids' work, which I thought was very decent of the owner.

Of course, the new technological toy would be irresistible to the young maids. Too often the butler would catch them going up and down in the lift on insignificant errands, wasting their time. Finally, his patience would run out, and he would announce that the next girl fooling around with the lift would receive a birching in front of all of the servants.

The girls would take this to heart, and do their utmost to avoid capture. They would play with the lift only when the butler was busy with the master or about his duties on the other side of the house. Two of the maids would decide to have a couple of trips up and down when they thought the butler was asleep.

A grave miscalculation, that. The butler's room was directly next to the lift shaft, and the girls' delighted giggles would carry perfectly through the void, even if they were careful not to stop on his floor. He would meet them in the scullery once they've had enough, frowning meaningfully.

Even before he said a word, they would know that nothing in the world would save them from the impending birching.

Another fine artefact in the contemporary Cragside is a sketch on the wall, and the bottom of the staircase leading to the plunge pool. It shows a Roman soldier, sword in hand (symbolism, duh) kneeling beside a cage. The cage is inhabited by a scantily clad young lady, who is weeping and stretching her hands out towards him through the bar.

I didn't notice a name for either the picture or the artist, but have had a fine few minutes trying to decide how the pretty girl could possibly have ended up in a cage, with her Roman lover on the outside. I'm still not sure what happened there, but I enjoyed creating a small traffic jam at the bottom of the steps while I studied it in detail.

The Cragside punishments

By Abel on 14 September 2008

Grand rooms, stories of maidservants, paintings of beautiful young wives on the walls – it's no wonder that, at some point when touring a country house, our minds flick into spanko overdrive. It's unusual, though, for it to happen quite as quickly as it did at Cragside, about which Haron's been posting recently. For no sooner than one has walked past the ticket desk do tour groups find themselves in the butler's pantry. And there, on the wall, are three carpet beaters – right next to a solid table over which girls would presumably have bent.

But matters become more complicated than that, for a few rooms further in is the butler's study: a comfortable room, this, complete with his writing desk, armchair and bowler hat. He'd come here in the evenings, no doubt, to relax and unwind at the end of a busy day – whilst still remaining alert should the gentlemen next door require a top-up of port.

Hold on, though. We'd just pictured the punishments in the pantry. And here was this other, quite wonderfully-evocative room. It would be such a shame to allow it to go to imaginary-waste. The solution was clear: the first room, the pantry would be for summary punishment – a few sharp, stinging swats of the carpet beater thwacking across the girl's dress in the middle of the day. But this second room, the study? The young maids would dread it, for this is where the butler would deal with more serious misbehaviour.

The girl would be told to wait outside his study, facing the wall, at the end of her day's work. No knocking to alert him to her presence: she'd wait for twenty minutes, more sometimes, until he happened to emerge and notice her. Once inside, she'd receive a stern lecture, before the cane would be taken from the top of his bookcase and she'd be told to undress and touch her toes. Six strokes, sometimes a dozen, would follow: hard, expertly-administered, a hard-learnt lesson.

And then... a few rooms further on... his Lordship's study. Far grander. Surely this couldn't go unused in our reinvention of the house? Conveniently, it stood at the top of stairs leading down to the Victorian sauna – complete with cold plunge pool. Ah, but the two rooms could easily be combined.

"Mr Watkins?"

"Yes, my Lord?"

"Would you take the girl downstairs and make sure she's clean?"

And the maid, caught committing some particularly dreadful offence (rifling through a guests' belongings, maybe?), would be led – protesting, no doubt – down the narrow stairs. Her clothes would be removed; she'd be ordered into the icy waters.

The butler would then dry her, roughly, with a towel before leading her – shivering, still naked, back up the stairs. His Lordship would be waiting, the birch cut by the butler that afternoon in his hand.

"You may leave us, Mr Watkins, whilst I deal with the girl." And the butler would wait outside, listening to her sobs. No short, sharp shock, this – his Lordship would flog her slowly, methodically, making every stroke count, giving her one final chance instead of dismissing her without references.

And then the door would open, and the girl would emerge – soundly thrashed – into the corridor, to be led back to the servants' quarters by the butler. She'd return under his supervision the following morning, of course, to kneel painfully on the floor, brush in hand, and sweep up the remnants of the birch that had scattered across the rugs during her punishment. And then nothing more would be spoken of the incident again.

The sultan's bathhouse

By Abel on 16 September 2008

I'm in Cyprus at the moment, staying with Cath and having a lovely time.

Yesterday, we went exploring in Nicosia, the capital, which is delightful. A little research had revealed a hidden gem, the Hamam Omerye, a traditional bathhouse. Dating from the 14th century, it's been restored recently, capturing a Europa Nostra award (Europe's top gong for conservation) in 2006. We were lucky, in that bathing is usually single-sex; Monday is the only "couples" day.

The place is a delight, a haven from the heat and bustle of the world outside – all fluffy towels and relaxing massages. The Hamam bath itself is a set of seven rooms, each at a different temperature; one sits (or lies) on the hot stone benches, unwinding, scrubbing oneself (or one's partner) gently in the warm waters. It's quite gorgeous.

Of course, as we relaxed, I told tale of the sultan in Ottoman times. The girls of his harem would have been sent here to bathe, no doubt. No towels to cover his young ladies in those days, of course; as a result, the marks of his displeasure would be plain to see, a lesson to all.

Yet one new girl had clearly not learnt said lesson: she'd displeased the sultan, and her fate awaited her: "You are to report to his chamber on your return from the bathhouse." She'd plead for his mercy, but she knew that none would be forthcoming. By tomorrow, she'd be the one wearing fresh stripes from his whip as she bathed naked with the others.

Submission

By Abel on 26 September 2008

I've rather grown to like Norwich over the years, especially since a lovely boutique hotel opened there, thus making my occasional work visits so much more comfortable.

Now, I've never done anything kinky in said hotel – so why it should appear as the setting for an extremely rude dream last night is quite beyond me.

It started in the restaurant; I was dining with a young lady I'd not met before, but one who I knew from correspondence to be kinkily-inclined. Our conversation became more intense as the meal progressed; by dessert it was known that I could expect her absolute submission and obedience in whatever was to follow.

We ordered coffee; I ordered her to remove her knickers. At the dinner table. She blushed, hesitated, wriggled as far as she could go under the table, obeyed. She handed them to me; I wouldn't take them. "Fold them neatly, and place them in front of you."

"But the waiter will see." He was returning, bearing our cappuccinos.

"Precisely."

I made her leave them there when we left the table. "Please let me take them..."

I ignored her pleas.

Upstairs, we reached the door to my room. I looked at her carefully, checking she was OK: she looked back, and smiled a smile of nervous validation.

No sooner had I closed the door behind us than I forced her up against the wall, my hand enjoying the absence of underwear.

"Do you like that, young lady?"

"Yes, sir."

I took my hand away, moved back. "Good. Then we shall continue. Once, that is, I've strapped you for your disobedience as we left the dinner table."

"But I didn't want to leave them there."

The slap across her face wasn't hard: it didn't need to be. It confirmed the order of things, and when I told her to strip naked and bend over the end of the bed, her compliance was immediate.

There followed much naughtiness, over which I'll draw a polite veil. But I am now rather looking forward to my next trip to that hotel.

The stowaway

By Abel on 28 September 2008

Dinner with Cath one evening last week was down by the quayside. We ate in a little fish restaurant – the sort of place where there's no menu, only the waitress appearing to reel off the list of the three types of fish they had that evening.

She forgot to tell us about that morning's incident, but we knew instinctively what had happened. The local girls had become quite a nuisance over the holidays, as they messed around on the fishing boats in the harbour – jumping from one to the other, hiding behind the nets, disappearing below deck. Only, none of the boats had ever set sail with one of the girls on board – until then.

The captain had found her, looking scared, when they were a half hour or so into their trip. He'd turned the boat straight around, of course, radioing back to the harbourmaster. It occurred to him as he unbuckled his belt that it was fortunate that the sea was calm enough for him to be able to land his strokes accurately as he whipped her on deck.

Her father – a local businessman – was waiting when they docked. No hugs: a curt "wait there" as he apologised to the fisherman and dug a selection of notes from his wallet to pay for the wasted time and fuel.

He pointed to a low, stone wall, ordering her to take down her jeans and knickers and bend over. He looked approvingly at the captain's handiwork, then folded his own belt double to add his own strokes to the punishment, as the crowd looked on.

After they'd all been to so much trouble, I'm pleased to report that the sea bass was quite excellent.

Will he tell Daddy?

By Haron on 3 October 2008

Walking down a London street, I saw a girl – seventeen years old or thereabouts – talking to a businessman in a crisp suit. He was smiling and affable. Her face was frozen in what she obviously hoped was an expression of polite interest, but her body language said plainly that she would be out of this conversation as soon as it was acceptable.

I think the businessman was her father's associate from work. He's been to dinner a few times, knows the girl very well. When she got onto the train this morning, heading for London instead of school, she had no idea she would walk into him while enjoying her stroll past swish shops.

She wanted to dash into a shop to hide, but he noticed and hailed her first. Will he tell Daddy that he saw her in the street? Would it be wise to tell him the truth, "My father doesn't know I'm in London today, please don't tell him." No, impossible; grown-ups have a bizarre unspoken agreement about these things.

What if she said, "Please don't tell Daddy you saw me; he'll going to give me a whipping if he knows I was in London today." No, that's pathetic; she can't let him know that she still gets spanked.

Act cool. Act polite. Act as though you're supposed to be here. He won't question it, or mention it to Daddy, or think about it at all five minutes after you part.

Caned in parallel

By Abel on 10 October 2008

Hotel bar the other night. The rather delightful lady at the next table turned to me and apologised for any disturbance that her charges were causing. They were on a school trip, she explained: "seeing Europe" in a month. In fact, the youngsters were impeccably behaved.

That said, one of her fellow teachers kept checking up on the whereabouts of some of the party. Were they under suspicion of sneaking out for a furtive cigarette, I wondered? Had any of them boldly ordered booze at the bar, to be smuggled upstairs?

My imagination ran riot later. He'd conduct a room check: the hotel would have issued him with a master key to open the various doors. He'd knock loudly before entering: even that wouldn't give Lisa and Vicky, two of the most senior girls, time to disperse the clouds of smoke, or hide the empty bottles.

They'd have been lectured at the start of the trip in no uncertain terms about the consequences of breaking the clearly-set-out rules. Reminded, on a regular basis. A 'final final' warning issued to all after some shenanigans the previous weekend in Paris: confirmation that the usual school punishments would apply for breaking the usual school regulations.

"I'm so very disappointed in you. Of all the girls I'd have imagined having to punish on this trip, you would have been the very last." He'd leave them for a moment, telling them that by the time he returned, he'd expect them to be in position to be caned. Kneeling on the bed beside each other. Shoulders down, arms outstretched, pyjama bottoms down and backsides up.

It would take him a few minutes – to find his cane, to find his female colleague, and for her in turn to find her cane.

The girls would be ready on their return: he'd position himself to the side of one, right-handed, whilst his left-handed fellow disciplinarian measured out the rattan from the far side of the other. "Smoking always results in six strokes of the cane," he'd remind them, before laying the first red strip across Lisa. His colleague would go next, paralleling his line across Vicky.

Then simultaneously. Then Vicky. Lisa. Simultaneous. Up to four each. He'd notice them holding hands: he'd choose to ignore it.

Vicky, Vicky. Lisa. Lisa.

He'd pause, allowing the girls a moment to try, in vain, to compose themselves. And then the best friends would hear the next dreaded sentence. "And drinking alcohol, too, always results in six strokes. Would you care to swap positions, Mrs Sandton?"

Tanned over the tannoy
By Abel on 14 October 2008

The impatient message over the loudspeakers cut through the quiet air in the bookstore:

Eva, call 251. Eva, please call 251.

But Eva was a naughty girl, for a few minutes later, the voice shrilled again, half weary, half annoyed:

Could Eva *please* call extension 251. Thank you.

She must have responded to this second call, for we were spared the third announcement:

Eva! Report immediately to the manager's office.

She hadn't called because she'd been afraid of the scolding that would inevitably follow. Not to have done so had made matters much, much worse. Downcast, she took the escalator up from the non-fiction section; went through the door marked 'Private'. Knocked, and was called in.

"And why didn't you call when you were asked to, young lady?"

"Because. Because... I'm sorry, sir."

The manager would make an example of her: the tannoy would be flicked back on before her punishment commenced. The sharp retort of the strap would echo six times across the building. Other assistants would wince at their friend's squeals, some remembering their own toe-touching moments. And the shoppers would look up from their browsing and realise quite how much effort went into maintaining the store's impeccable reputation for quality.

Preparing for the public flogging
By Haron on 15 October 2008

Abel left me in our hotel room to go to a work appointment. I stuck my head out of the window to watch him leave, and noticed that the hotel ballroom, directly underneath me, was being prepared for some kind of event: a red carpet unrolled, a couple of TV vans parked outside, barriers set up to keep the onlookers from spilling onto the reserved area.

I wondered if this would be how a town square would be prepared for a public flogging.

I didn't foresee a red carpet for that occasion, of course, but there would be a temporary explosion of activity around the normally lonely whipping post.

A barrier would certainly be erected, leading all the way from the door of the jail opposite. The TV vans would be here early, trying to glimpse the arrival of the executioner for work, still in his street clothes and looking safe and normal.

And, I think, there would be a small contingent of long-time fans, the type of folks who make it their business to be present at every flogging, no matter how rare. They would bicker politely over the best spots in that sliver of space where not only can you see the lash land onto the exposed buttocks and back, but where you can catch a glimpse of the agony on the convict's face.

The convict – me, of course – would be watching all this from a tiny barred window in the jail cell. There would be a clock on the wall, too, counting down the minutes until it's time to make that walk along the path between the barriers, under the glare of TV lights. Towards the whipping post. Towards the executioner, no longer casual-looking in his sleeveless shirt with sweatbands and biceps exposed.

Towards the lash.

A Parisian spanking
By Abel on 16 October 2008

Haron was whisked off on Sunday for a surprise birthday day-trip to Paris on the Eurostar.

We gawped at Notre Dame. We wandered round a museum – an old prison, full of kinky potential even if the French were wont to favour "off with their heads" over sound judicial birchings. We bought naughty antique postcards from the stalls on the banks of the Seine.

We argued over the glass pyramid in the Louvre courtyard; I'll leave you to guess which of us was the more traditional, and hence outraged by its modernity. We strolled through the Tuileries, admiring the local scenery.

And we ate. Oh, what a lunch! A tiny, stumbled-upon-in-a-backstreet French brasserie; hearty provincial food, of the very highest order.

Our waitress was quite delightful, which inevitably led Haron and I to start whispering pervy thoughts to each other. She nearly knocked over our water: we imagined the proprietaire noting her misdemeanour on a sheet behind the counter, from which her errors would be tallied at the end of the week.

And then: a crash, and she sent a glass on the neighbouring table tumbling to the ground. There were some offences, we decided, that would not wait until the week was out. He'd beckon her into his tiny office, and take the strap from the wall. There'd scarcely be enough room to swing it, but his arm and aim would be practiced. She'd yelp, and cry, and apologise, and be hugged, and appear to serve our dessert with tears still in her eyes.

(Actually, she just got out a dustpan and brush and cheerfully cleared up the mess. Quite disappointing, really!)

Now calling at Correctional Institute
By Abel on 30 October 2008

Alighting from the Victoria Line at Green Park recently, it struck me that the Queen must be a forgetful old dear. After all, the announcer greets each train with, "Change here for Buckingham Palace," presumably in case Her Majesty (a) happens to be on board, and (b) can't remember the way home.

Helpful tube announcements could extend to other stations, now I think of it.

Take that little-known stop on the Metropolitan Line: Correctional Institute Station. "Alight here for the Royal Disciplinary Service", the tannoy proclaims. Passengers peer curiously from the windows at the scared girls who disembark, heading towards their punishments – to be replaced in the carriages by the latest batch of freshly-flogged young ladies who, tears in their eyes, refuse kind offers of a seat.

Running for the train
By Abel on 3 November 2008

The girl ran at full pelt across the bridge in Central Station, holding her boyfriend's hand as they ran. The 16:3 was still in the platform: perhaps they might still make it?

They were half way down the stairs (taken two at a time) when the guard's whistle sounded. We glimpsed them again on the platform, moments later, pleading for him to revoke his order, praying that the electric doors would slide open once more and let them on board. But it was too late: the train had started to glide from the platform on its journey north. She turned to her boyfriend, and buried her head against his shoulder; he hugged her, as the tears started to flow.

For her father knew that the library closed at one. He'd warned her last week when she'd returned home so late, and not for the first time – clearly suspicious as to how she might have passed so much time alone in the city. A final warning, ominous in implication.

And three hours could – just – have been explained away, had he been in a good mood. The library stayed open a little longer; she had to grab some lunch; there was a book she needed to look at in Waterstone's. The previous train had been delayed, cancelled; hers had broken down, been subject to failing signals. (Surely he wouldn't phone the train company to check?)

But the extra hour? She knew full well the implication, and the thought of daddy's unforgiving belt was almost too much to bear...

PS actually, they caught the train, but you know how our minds work!!!

Reality spanking

By Abel on 9 November 2008

Sometimes my imagination wanders into very dark places indeed. I developed a reality TV show concept in my sleep a few weeks ago, for example, and have been toying ever since with whether or not to blog it. The sort of thing I've shared with Haron, and a couple of friends, all of whom have grimaced, paused, and then given a guilty smile and a "It shouldn't be. But that's hot."

The inspiration's fairly clear – a cross between 'V for Vendetta' and 'Sulphuric Acid' (a remarkable, disturbing, brilliant novel by Belgian author Amelie Nothomb), mixed with the dawn of this year's Freshers' weeks around the country.

At the start of my dream, one of said new students is kidnapped, and taken to a dark, windowless room. Unbeknownst to her, her movements are being observed by a myriad of hidden cameras, broadcasting live to the nation. She's well looked after – other, of course, than having been deprived of her freedom. Food is passed in to her at regular intervals, the staff check on her regularly. Uncannily, the books they also provide are just to her taste – almost as if someone had been observing her closely before snatching her from the street.

It's the second evening's broadcast that offers the viewers their first chance to join in. They'd been shown pictures of the punishment chamber. The various implements had been displayed, explained. The early show allowed them to vote: "Choose your implement now. Call or send a text message now!

The method of punishment duly selected (and the option of 'No punishment' having been soundly rejected), the later edition that evening allowed the general public to choose the number of strokes. Live on TV, the young woman would thus be stripped, showered, taken to the punishment room, and thrashed according to public demand.

The series would comprise more than just floggings; other tortures would be on offer too for the viewers' delectation and the girl's torment. Until, eventually, the public were bored of her: one night, the option to 'Choose another girl' would be offered. The incumbent would be abandoned, dazed and confused, at some remote roadside; the producers would set off to capture their next unwitting star.

The scary spanking cult

By Haron on 12 November 2008

I dreamed I was an FBI agent infiltrating a cult. The cult leader was the head of an adopted family of over 50 adults and children, and ran the whole thing with an iron fist – or with many leather implements, anyway.

My role was to join the happy cult family, and do whatever was required of me as I gathered evidence for a prosecution. Having recently joined, I was on the bottom rung of the family hierarchy, treated essentially as a maid, threatened with punishment at every turn.

I woke up just as the family assembled for a Saturday review of everybody's behaviour, where I knew I would be held on the back on one of my "brothers" and whipped with a wide leather strap. In the dream, this fate was terrifying, but I was rather disappointed, upon waking, to have missed it.

Getting used to spanking

By Haron on 14 November 2008

Abel has this idea – born, no doubt, out of his inexperience at being on the receiving end of corporal punishment – that when you go for a while without being spanked, the first punishment you receive hurts you more than if you were spanked on a regular basis.

The natural conclusion from the above is that if you get spanked often, you feel less pain when you do. That's just not true for me: my naturally low pain threshold doesn't get any higher if I play every day; if anything, I experience pain even more keenly after being "pre-spanked", if you will. Frequent spanking doesn't do a thing to help me process the pain better. Whether I got spanked yesterday or three weeks ago, the next spanking is going to hurt exactly the same.

This seems to disappoint Abel. When I came home from my last stay with my parents, he was raring to give me a hard six-of-the-best without any warm up, on the basis that on my unspanked posterior it would feel close to an authentic schoolgirl experience. I'm all for authenticity, but I had to explain that it would hurt just the same as if he'd been merrily spanking me all week long. Although he believes me intellectually, I don't think he can accept this in his perverted heart.

I hope it doesn't mean that in the course of our spanking life he canes me harder because he feels I'm used to it, and therefore need to take more to feel it. I really don't need to be caned hard to be impressed. Perhaps I should set Abel lines: "My wife cannot get used to pain. My wife cannot get used to pain."

I wonder if my constant wimpiness is universal. What do you think? Does a spanking hurt you more if you haven't played for a while? Does it hurt less if you've been particularly active?

P.S. I did get an extremely hard six-of-the-best on my first night back, of course. Abel very kindly agreed to warm me up – with a dozen strokes of a hairbrush. I'm sure he thought it helped.

Selling Daddy's paddle
By Haron on 18 November 2008

An implement hunt on eBay has once again proved that a few well-chosen search words can get you pretty much any source of pain you may wish for.

I imagine that one paddle in particular was offered up by someone other than its rightful owner. The girl's

Daddy is away on business, but he's had a call from school about her slipping behaviour.

"It's the paddle for you, young lady," he told her. "As soon as I get home on Friday." With a few days to spare, she makes a swift decision: her father's paddle is up on eBay, with a cute description of its 'novelty value' and a friendly price tag. Within a day, it's gone.

Daddy comes back to discover the loss. He doesn't buy the girl's protestations that she hasn't the *slightest* idea where the paddle has disappeared to. He proves to her that a father's chief implement is always with him, as he turns her over his knee for a scorching interrogation. Weeping, she admits to the theft.

"Very well," Daddy sighs. "In that case we will have to bid on a new paddle. Your original punishment is deferred until it arrives. And in the meantime, you're grounded. You have earned yourself a bedtime spanking every day from now until the day the matter is resolved. Go and change into your pyjamas now; we shall start right away."

Details, details

By Abel on 29 November 2008

How strange. My dream last night was incredibly clear. The slate floor was covered in sawdust. The girl's ankles were pale, slim, bare: I held them tight as I bound her into position for her flogging. She was obedient, compliant, as if resigned to her fate.

Only – and here's what surprised me – she was being held down by iron shackles. Heavy, old. She winced at the cold as the metal made contact with her skin. No doubt she'd be wincing and writhing for other reasons within moments.

Surprising? Well, it struck me that I don't think I've ever pictured metal cuffs before: my dream girls have always been strapped down with leather binds, tied with rope. But metal? I rather like the idea: I might have to browse eBay later.

Depressing, too, as I think about it. Because that was the sum total of the dream: ankles, not a whole girl. Shackles, not the entire whipping frame. Fixing into her position, not the punishment itself. Still, it was so vivid that I have a very pleasant picture in my mind to carry me through the busy day ahead...

Caned no matter what
By Haron on 2 December 2008

Abel and I were standing on a train platform in the middle of a rush hour. Opposite us there stood a smartly dressed, very pretty young lady, who was contentedly munching on something.

Abel turned to me: "If I were her father, I'd cane her for chewing gum in public."

"Do you know," I said, "I think she's just eating a chocolate bar."

A short pause, as he contemplated this. "Oh well. I'd just cane her anyway."

The long arm of the law
By Abel on 9 December 2008

The Independent reports that the Metropolitan Police are to launch a series of gift products:

"From early next year, the toy makers John Adams will sell New Scotland Yard-branded children's forensic science sets, complete with fingerprint dust."

I promise you now that Haron's prints are going to be found by the investigating officer, who will then take her away to be punished with one of the:

"reproduction cat o' nine tails, birches and punishment straps that will form part of the new range."

OK, I may be making up that last part. But I am fascinated to know what may be discovered amidst the 15,000 artefacts in the Met's historical collection. "It is housed in a warehouse, but with the funds raised from the various licensing deals, the police hope to be able to put it in a museum for members of the public to see." Sounds as if that would be worth a visit!

Reformatory floggings

By Abel on 13 December 2008

A night of reformatory floggings; I became a Governor in my dreams last night.

First, I found myself showing some distinguished visitor around our facilities. We had stopped outside a door, and were peering through the glass window, watching the scene inside.

A young, uniformed, female officer – in her late twenties? – was circling around the punishment frame. Holding a birch. A pale girl was tied to a frame, quite naked. The upturned U of the frame presented her body to us from the side, perfectly symmetrical; her wrists and ankles were tied tight. It appeared that her flogging was just about to begin.

I turned to my guest, and explained that the officer concerned was one of our best. "You see, she was an inmate here herself when she was younger. I think we helped her to see the error of her ways. I had to whip her when she was here, you know: I'm sure she's more effective at giving out punishments now having been on the receiving end herself."

Sadly, the dream faded. But later, another young prison officer was seen waiting in a different punishment room. She was a trainee: the regulations demanded that she must 'demonstrate her competence in the administration of corporal punishment' as part of attaining her qualifications. Our system was simple: as the young officers drew near to their graduation, they would therefore be asked to act as the Punishment Officer for a random girl who'd broken the regulations. Under supervision, of course: the examiner stood to the side of the room, with his clipboard.

A prisoner was marched in. The door was bolted shut; her handcuffs unlocked. And a look of panic crossed the young officer's face. For this was no random prisoner: this was a girl who she knew, who she liked, who she'd comforted and cuddled and helped through her sentence.

The examiner looked at the officer: "Read out the charge sheet." (Refusing to return to her cell when instructed; lashing out at the guards who had come to take her away).

"And what punishment do the statutes lay down for those offences?"

"Eight to twelve strokes for refusing to return to her cell, sir. Twelve to eighteen for striking an officer, sir."

"And what is your assessment in this case?"

"It states on the form that it is her first offence, sir. So I would see no reason to administer more than the minimum in each case. Twenty strokes in total, sir."

"Very good. And what implement should be used?"

The officer looked down at the charge sheet, but knew already. "She's nineteen, sir. So the senior prison cane."

"Indeed." The young officer walked to the corner of the room, unlocked the cupboard, took out the cane. And then looked at the prisoner, whose eyes pleaded for mercy, and ordered her to strip...

(Sadly, this dream too then faded before the administration of the punishment. But I'm sure we can imagine the rest...)

A vote for punishment
By Haron on 14 December 2008

This weekend we have a friend staying, whom we'll call L. Yesterday the three of us settled down to watch the final of the talent show X-Factor, when Abel announced that we would have a bet riding on the results.

"If Alexandra wins, you girls will get no punishment at all. If GLS win, it's six strokes each, and if Eoghan wins, you get twelve each. Clear?"

It was pretty clear that Abel didn't like Eoghan very much.

L and I agreed and crossed our fingers for Alexandra, and squirmed our way all through the hours and hours of singing. We supported her so fervently, that I'm sure her victory was caused as much by our channelling of good thoughts as by the voting of the Great British public.

A well-deserved victory, L and I agreed.

Lest you think Abel is getting soft, what with giving us the option of no punishment at all, I must add that in the interval L got her first birching, which looked pretty painful; I then had a mini-birching with what was left of the rods.

Still, the X-factor bet? We won. Thanks, Alexandra.

The Christmas round-robin
By Abel on 23 December 2008

We received one of those horrible documents inserted into a Christmas card the other day, in which a vanilla acquaintance described the travails of their past twelve months in immensely boring detail.

I started giggling after a few moments, though, and Haron asked why. "Just imagine if these things were really honest," I said. Like...

Our garden was particularly lovely this spring. The joyous sense of spiritual renewal at this time of year was clouded, though, when Sophie was called before her housemaster for truancy and given her first caning.

Sadly, the three strokes he administered across her skirt were insufficient to drive home the message, for she found herself back in his study in October for a further taste of corporal punishment. This time, he gave her six of the best on the bare, and we are pleased to report that her conduct has been impeccable ever since.

2008 spanks for Jesus's birthday
By Haron on 26 December 2008

The true meaning of Christmas was not forgotten in our household yesterday. It was Jesus's birthday, right?
　　Don't worry, Jesus. Abel has delivered your birthday spanking to our guest Catherine and me, all 2008 swats and one to grow on.
　　rubs extremely tender bottom
　　Here's how it went:
　　Most spanks were no more than gentle taps.
　　But some were definitely not. (Hence, certain difficulty sitting down today.)
　　The swats were spread throughout the day – we started off before breakfast, and finished just as it was time for good girls to be tucked in bed.
　　Abel got one smack.
　　The cat got ten. (She purred her way through.)
　　Every casual swat delivered to a passing behind counted towards the final tally.
　　The implements came out for certain sections of the birthday spanking. There was a hairbrush, a new razor strop I gave Abel for Christmas (silly me), a carpet beater,

a soft flogger, a martinet, a bamboo swagger stick and a cane.

After we were done, Abel needed a serious shoulder rub to alleviate repetitive strain pain in his shoulder. Though that might have been from all the cooking.

And then there was more whipping – just because.

The strokes of the new year
By Abel on 31 December 2008

There were thirty or so of them at St. Mary's to see in the New Year. Their families lived abroad – posted far and wide on behalf of Her Majesty or for some multinational corporation. Some of the girls had flown home for Christmas, but headed back to England early. Other parents had travelled here for the festivities with their daughters, but pressures of work had dragged them back to far-flung climes as soon as Boxing Day had passed.

The girls been allowed to stay up late. A pyjama-clad picnic in the sixth-form common room was the order of the night; after all, the catering staff weren't going to come in to cook when they could be celebrating in the pub. Music was turned up loud; they sang, danced, hugged, counted down the minutes towards midnight. And then the headmaster had walked in. Smiling, festive. Until he'd noticed the bottle of vodka.

–

She waited in the dark corridor, alone. She was cold, her dressing gown too thin to keep out the end-of-year chill in the near-empty school.

She could hear their laughter in the distance, and then the cheers. It must be midnight: the new year had come.

He'd be here in a moment, once he'd wished the others well for the coming twelve months. "You, of all people, should understand the rules about alcohol," he'd said. Prefects should set an example, he'd added. She knew the punishment. She should go and wait outside his study.

How many would he give her? Four? Six? Would he permit her the modesty of her dressing gown, her pyjama bottoms, or punish her on the bare? Over his desk (like the only other time she'd been here to be punished, two years before), or bent over touching her toes?

She heard footsteps; stood up straight. "Ah, Emma," he exclaimed, as he fumbled in a pocket for his keys. "Come in. Let's get this over with quickly, shall we?"

—

We hope you like our little end of year story – and enjoy your new year's celebrations this evening, wherever you may be. We wish you every happiness for 2009!

2009

Spanking in his sleep

By Haron on 3 January 2009

One night last week we took a late train home, and we were both shattered. Abel was the first to go to sleep, looking as innocent as though he'd never spanked a girl in his life.

Almost. Because pretty soon he started to murmur something, holding an animated (but unintelligible) conversation with somebody in the dreamland.

This was pretty funny and endearing, and quiet enough that I didn't feel the need to wake him up. I did wonder what I'd do if all of a sudden he started waving his hands, and coming out with things like "You are a very badly behaved young lady, bend over and touch your toes at once."

Actually, for all I know, that's exactly what he'd been saying anyway. He just wasn't loud enough to frighten anybody else in the carriage.

Birching the Tudor ladies
By Abel on 6 January 2009

We visited the Tower of London over the Christmas holidays – an easy way to entertain my parents for a couple of hours, despite the crowds.

The black history of the place is all around, from the block and axe in the White Tower, past the place of execution, to the grave of Lady Jane Grey in the chapel.

And then there was the Birching Green*, to cheer us all up. The Tudor nobility, needless to say, weren't awfully keen on mingling with the lower classes. This extended to the punishment of any crimes that the aristocracy might commit.

Lady Mary Bradgate, for example, was the youngest daughter of the Marquess of Devon. During a stay in London, she and her cousin, Lady Elizabeth Dudley, took their carriage to The Exchange. There, they asked a shopkeeper to see some silk handkerchiefs, which he laid out before them on the counter. They then tried on a number of fashionable hats, one of which Lady Mary purchased.

Within moments of their departure, however, a commotion ensued. As the shopkeeper returned the handkerchiefs to the drawer, he'd noticed that the most expensive was missing. The constable was called and was given a description of the (highly unusual) pattern on the silk, which had only arrived in London the previous day.

Without further ado, the constable set off for the Marquess's townhouse. By the time the young women had finished their shopping and returned home in their carriage, he was in deep conversation with the Marquess. The girls were called into the library; the situation explained. Both pleaded their innocence. A bell was rung; their maids appeared.

"Would you leave us for a moment?" the Marquess asked the constable. And then the maids were ordered to strip their mistresses and search for the missing silk.

Lady Mary's guilt was quickly established, and the magistrate called. The option of a trial in the courthouse, followed – no doubt – by a whipping at Newgate was clearly not acceptable for a young noblewoman, and so arrangements were put in place: "You will report to the Tower one hour after sunrise tomorrow morning, and there you will be whipped."

A sleepless, tearful night ensued. Her cousin and maid accompanied her on the journey, but could offer little consolation. They were taken to the Beauchamp Tower; Lady Mary was made to change from her fine clothes into a plain, rough dress, before the guard arrived to take her out to the Green in front. The whipping frame was already in place; the Yeoman bade her bend forward, and tied her tightly in position, before taking the first of the birches. He called forward Lady Elizabeth, asking her to lift her cousin's skirt and bare her for her punishment.

Her howls echoed around the Tower, and out through the cold morning air to the boats on the river outside, as the strokes rained down. The first rod lasted around fifteen strokes; the second a mere dozen, before a third birch was taken to complete the forty that made up the allotted tally. And then she was untied, led back to change back into her finery, and marched from the Tower for the most uncomfortable of carriage rides home.

–

* Actually, there wasn't. But there should have been.

Reviewing the situation
By Abel on 10 January 2009

"Oliver!", now previewing at the Theatre Royal Drury Lane, has to be one of the very best musicals to arrive in London for years. The direction is superb; the choreography (by the ever-wonderful Matthew Bourne) simply breathtaking. The set is remarkable, and the cast – led by the brilliant Rowan Atkinson as Fagin – top-notch. Beg, borrow or steal a ticket...

But actually... whilst I'm talking about stealing: there is one flaw in the production. See, it's that Dickens chap. All of the pickpockets in his book were lads. Why on earth didn't he write a part for a female thief? No imagination.

I can picture the scene now – before Oliver meets the Artful Dodger for the first time. We're introduced to Fagin's motley crew as they cower at the back of the crowd, watching as one of their number, Margaret, is tied to a post and thrashed for stealing a stallholder's wallet. The punishment officer would sing heartily as he laid on the strokes: 'The Whipping Song' would be the most popular in the whole show.

The young woman would be seen with the other gang members later, still rubbing her backside. There'd be no faking the flogging, with the audience just a few feet away, but hers wouldn't be a speaking role – so a different actress could be brought in every night from the local theatre schools to suffer, whilst fulfilling her ambition of appearing on the West End stage.

In trouble with the choirmaster
By Haron on 11 January 2009

In my dream I was singing in the school choir. It was a final rehearsal before a concert at an open day; I was awfully nervous.

Just as the choirmaster raised his conductor's wand to direct us to start, I knew I couldn't remember a single word of the song. I was in complete panic, while he noticed at once, despite there being fifty other girls in the choir.

"You," he stabbed at me with the wands. "Sing it on your own."

Heart freezing in my chest, I explained that I was having a temporary memory glitch. I couldn't remember the words. He looked thunderous.

"Out of the room," he hissed.

"Please, sir," said one of the other girls. "She'll remember them when we all start singing."

I promised I would, and unexpectedly he relented. "Very well. You can stay and sing. But after the rehearsal, see me for your punishment."

I knew I would be caned when I went to see him, but I didn't mind: I could stay and sing with all the other girls.

I don't remember whether I did get caned or not. Knowing dream logic, he probably fed me tea and cakes instead. Which would be completely fine with me – and quite nice if it happened in real life as well!

Night-time dialogue
By Haron on 15 January 2009

Abel (murmuring sleepily, and only half-way coherently): "I have a question."

Haron (only a little more coherently): "Yes?"

Abel: "In the olden days, when everybody lived in black-and-white... When a maid got caned, did she have grey stripes?"
Haron: "Yes, dear."
Abel: "That makes sense."

Schoolgirl against teacher
By Haron on 21 January 2009

Last weekend I played schoolgirl again, sitting down to lessons with a small group of friends, revelling in a day of unabashed naughtiness. Although the classroom experience is not new to me, there are always moments of sharp mental pleasure that I can file away as some of my treasured memories.

This time, the day was spiced up with several encounters with one of our three teachers, Mr Basford (also known as my good friend Richard). To the intense discomfort of my schoolgirl alter-ego Sylvie Barnable, he taught art. I'm not just bad at art – I'm inept to a catastrophic degree. After trying for a couple of minutes to master the shading trick that looked so easy when other people were doing it, I gave up. I could earnestly try and fail, or I could just draw something unrelated and borderline obscene in the corner of my sheet, and get into trouble.

It didn't take Mr Basford too long to notice what I still claim was a cannon (to illustrate our previous lesson on Napoleonic wars). He called me to the centre of the room and administered a quick, efficient strapping. I'm not good with straps, but I took it as valiantly as I could, and returned to my place. "Barnable, if you don't try, you won't get better," Mr Basford said. "If you don't pick up your pencil and work, I will cane you."

I didn't want to be caned right then, and I felt uncomfortable being the centre of attention, so I did pick up my pencil. I also moaned and knocked my head against the wall several times, just to express how unlikely I thought any progress in my artistic skills was. I didn't expect for a second to get into trouble for this small act of rebellion, but Mr Basford immediately told me to come back into the centre of the room. "But sirrr," I whined, "I was going to do it, I was!" I thought I was surely in for a caning now, and was glad of the brief strapping that would serve as a warm-up. However, I was ready to take it in my stride.

Instead, Richard did something that completely undid me: he placed a chair in the middle of the room, and told me to bend over his lap. My 16-year-old alter ego was struck dumb with the embarrassing horror of it: it's hardly ever done, spanking a girl over the knee in the classroom, in front of all her friends. "Please, sir," I whispered, begging uselessly. The teacher was unrelenting, and over his lap I went, half-cringing with embarrassment, half-faint with pleasure from being so expertly derailed.

The spanking was stingy, brisk. I couldn't help whimpering and squirming around. Richard is a tall man, and I'm a small girl, so my feet didn't touch the ground; I felt very high up and vulnerable – and when he picked up a small wooden paddle, I abandoned all thought of dignity. It stung a lot, and I kicked a lot, and it just went on stinging. Overall I didn't take it very well, and by the time the ordeal was over, I didn't even care.

I was only starting to pull myself together when the next lesson began. All through the day, the girls took turns to be sent out of the classroom for private interviews with one of the free teachers, to pay for random sins committed (or concocted) previously. I'd completely forgotten my turn was coming up soon, but when the immaculate Miss Marwood arrived to teach us etiquette, she produced a pink slip and read it out. "Sylvie Barnable, report to Mr Basford."

My jaw fell. "Oh, fuck," I blurted, clutching my head, and knew at once what I'd done, and my heart nearly stopped. At least it got a laugh out of my classmates.

"But first, come out here and bend over," said Miss Marwood without skipping a beat. "I won't tolerate profanity in my classroom."

Thus it was that I arrived at the private punishment session with Mr Basford with my bottom stinging from a freshly delivered dose of the strap.

Here, he continued his effective campaign of making me feel as vulnerable as possible. My sin was lack of effort in my studies, which, he said, was blatantly obvious from my conduct at his lesson. Where otherwise I might have gone for a "But sir, I'm trying!" defence, here I was trapped and exposed: clearly, as witnessed by the art lesson, I hadn't been trying at all. "Take off your skirt and knickers, you won't need them for a while," said Mr Basford, pushing aside the magnificent whipping bench, and picking up a chair, clearly intent on continuing our conversation from ten minutes before. "You seem hardened to the cane now, Barnable, so let's see what we can achieve with a good spanking."

If I'd had any fight left in me, any insolence, a stray smart remark – they were all gone now. I'm surprised I didn't burst into tears – but that was, perhaps, because in the background I couldn't help purring with pleasure of being so deftly played. I bent over his lap, and sighed forlornly as I saw my toes leave the floor. He pushed my back down, getting me bent all the way over, and resolutely clamped his right leg over both of mine. "There's been too much kicking from you," he said, thus securing me in place.

I can't describe the sheer delicious terror of being so intimately immobilised. The most secure handcuffs can't compare with warm physicality of an arm around my waist and a leg over the back of my knees. I was disarmed, turned into a small, submissive thing ready to repent my sins and promise nothing but stellar behaviour. The spanking, when it came, was firm, but still light enough that I could focus on my helplessness, fully savour my predicament. It didn't grow truly uncomfortable at any point, although it hurt just enough for me to struggle, squirm and yelp to my heart's content. And I did.

Eventually, there was a caning to finish off my punishment, and Mr Basford had been right: I would normally be well equipped to shrug it off – but I was still feeling small, and vulnerable, and very much susceptible to discipline. It was a good, solid full stop, though: something familiar to bring me back into senses. Sharp, clean pain of the rattan to wake me up and send me back to class almost myself again.

I don't think I was meant to enjoy my punishment quite so much.

The prefect, punished

By Abel on 24 January 2009

A gaggle of giggling girls joined the bus this morning, and piled into the back rows for a couple of miles of exuberant misbehaviour. Pretend-scuffles broke out; the gravest insults were shouted. The peace of the other passengers was quite shattered by the rowdy mob.

One girl stood aside from the others, though, in her grey skirt, black blazer, neatly-tied tie and immaculately-polished black shoes. She bore a badge on her lapel: 'Prefect'.

She would be the pupil called in to see the headmaster later in the day, after he'd taken the call from the transport company's boss. The Head read from his notes as the girl stood in front of his desk: "repeated misbehaviour"; "not at all acceptable"; "a disgrace"; "you assured me that the girls had been given a final warning".

"Please could you explain why you deem it to be appropriate to stand idly by, rather than carrying out your role as a Prefect?"

She could not.

He cleared the small pile of papers from the corner of the desk, and bade her bare and bend over – prefects, on those rare occasions they were caned, were always punished on the bare. Her first taste of corporal punishment in her up-to-now-impeccable school career: four strokes, taken bravely, through her tears. And then she was dismissed, and sent back to class.

Loving the punishment
By Haron on 25 January 2009

In my dream last night I was a lady's maid to a beautiful, demanding woman.

When she was interviewing me for the position, she said: "I have only two requirements: that you love me, and that you love being punished by me. Everything else flows from that."

I didn't quite understand at the time what she meant. I was quite prepared to be devoted to her needs, and it was easy to become fond of her. But at one point I was tidying her jewellery, and allowed two strings of pearls to get tangled. My mistress caught me trying to untangle them again, and immediately became annoyed.

"Fetch me a hairbrush," she commanded. "Right now."

When she saw tears spring to my eyes, she was even more angry: "Did I not say you were to love being punished by me? I will see some proper gratitude as I spank you."

And so, as she spanked me, she insisted that I smiled, and afterwards, she made me describe to her how wonderful it was to receive discipline from her hand.

And you know what? It was rather good, in fact.

Have a break

By Abel on 29 January 2009

I nearly choked on my toast at breakfast this morning. An advert appeared on the TV for Kit Kat. As I drooled at the thought of chocolate, the voiceover proudly announced the brand's new prize competition: "You could win your dream holiday."

Really?

I mean, really?

OK. So there'd be the limo to take me to the airport. A school bus would draw up at the terminal at the same time; the twenty or so kinky girls who'd be joining me on vacation would step off, and line up for a uniform inspection.

We'd fly first class, of course. The luxury resort would be perfect: we'd have the run of the place to ourselves. There'd be lessons and spankings and fine dining and spankings. And the hotel maids would have to be on their very best behaviour, lest they too found themselves over my knee.

And all for the price of a chocolate biscuit...

A broad hint

By Haron on 31 January 2009

This morning our cat went to the pile of canes, picked one up by the handle, and with much difficulty dragged it to me as I was getting out of bed.
I'm trying to figure out what she was trying to tell me.

Choosing a cane

By Haron on 6 February 2009

Yesterday morning I made an awful transgression which, Abel decided, merited an immediate punishment. So he sent me upstairs with the words, "Choose a cane and wait for me!"
Choose a cane. Easy for him to say. We have hundreds of them, one nastier than the other. How am I supposed to pick which one I fancy being striped with?
Generally, I prefer the thick, thuddy ones. They're cool. But they look so bloody scary, even if I know in my head that I really do like them. Then there are the whippy ones, which look, well, harmless – on account of their thinness – but I know pretty well the little bastards slice into you like a razor.
And then there are the dragon canes, which are whippy and thuddy at once, and are really not very good for anything but scaring a girl to death, but I *like* being scared to death.
So how can I just go and choose?
Anyway, I picked a thinnish cane we haven't used for a while, mainly because we haven't used it for a while. I thought it might be getting bored, and felt sorry for it.
I'm sure it felt a lot better after biting me six times in quick succession. That's what canes like to do, I think.

Punishing the posh girls

By Abel on 8 February 2009

The young ladies sitting opposite us on the train, late on Friday afternoon, were casually dressed – but expensively so – and their haircuts cost more than my suit. Their accents were pure top-drawer; their folders revealed them to be pupils at a particularly prestigious girls' boarding school.

The discussion turned to the fate awaiting some of their fellow students:

"Surely they won't be suspended for having cigarettes?"

"No," I leant over and replied. "The Headmistress will cane them on Monday morning – having left them to fret about their punishment over the weekend." (Only I didn't, of course. And she wouldn't!)

One of their number looked particularly concerned for her friends. "I went pale when they said there'd be an inspection. Thank goodness they didn't catch *me*." ("No, young lady, they didn't. But I shall be writing to your Headmistress this evening..."?)

Remembering punishments past

By Abel on 12 February 2009

An amusing scene in our favourite second-hand bookshop on our most recent visit. A rather distinguished older gentleman was sitting at the table in the middle of the store, browsing a pile of learned tomes. The young woman walking past stopped, the look of recognition on her face quickly followed by a deep blush.

"Hello, Flora. What a pleasant coincidence."

"Hello, sir."

It was the "sir" that caught my attention. So why was she blushing? Was she taken straight back to his study at school, recalling his housemasterly disappointment in her, remembering his sympathetic voice uttering the words she'd been dreading: "I am afraid that you really leave me no choice but to cane you."

Or did her memories stem from a poor school report – for a girl of her calibre – at the end of her first term in the Lower Sixth: "Flora really must apply more self-discipline if she is to achieve the high standards of which she is capable." Only... her uncle had decided that self-discipline might not suffice, and had arranged for her to visit a gentleman tutor twice a week.

Was it those Monday and Thursday visits that Flora now recalled in the bookstore, and the methods he had employed? Did her hands smart from the memory of his tawse? Did she picture herself standing before him in her school uniform, in his drawing room? Did she remember the look on his face as he discarded her essay ("B+. Should be more careful."), wince at the firmly-spoken line: "You may be content with second-rate work, Flora. Your uncle is not, and neither am I. You will remove your skirt, and bend over and touch your toes."

On a news-stand near you

By Abel on 16 February 2009

Bored, on a station, killing time before a train, browsing the magazines in WH Smith. And what a choice! 'The World of Cross-Stitching', 'Practical Fishkeeping', 'Tattoo', 'What Plasma & LCD TV' – and, this being Scotland, 'Tawse Monthly'.

I browsed the contents of the last of these with particular interest. A photographic feature showed the interior of John J Dick's Lochgelly shop. The

'Reminiscences' column featured one Aileen McStuart, still full of remorse at her visit to the headmaster for three strokes on each hand for smoking in the early 80s.

'Tried and Tested' reviewed the latest reproduction XHs available on eBay. Advice on caring for your strap appeared in the 'Hints and Tips' pages. Letters debated the use of the tawse at home – several young ladies describing strict regimes under the tutelage of Edinburgh governesses. And the Fiction section comprised a marvellous short story, in which poor Caitrin found herself bent over the end of her bed for a sound thrashing from her father.

Sadly for me, a rather pretty young lass wearing a tartan skirt pushed past me and snatched the last copy from before my very eyes, as I reached for my wallet to make a purchase. I can only assume that her father had given her strict instruction that morning to make sure she picked up his monthly copy on her way home from school. Had he found out about her rudeness, I dread to think what fate might have befallen her later that evening.

Lessons in deportment

By Haron on 18 February 2009

In "English Girlhood at School" Dorothy Gardiner quotes some ancient rules for the behaviour of young ladies:

> Clement of Alexandria [wrote]: "In conditions of luxury and excess, Christians must be distinguished by moderation and self-control... Even immoderate laughter is a snare to young girls; it distorts their faces, and may easily win them a bad name; a smile is all that is permissible."

The ideal picture of a Christian maid's deportment is borrowed from Zeno of Citium: "She must be pure of countenance, neither her brows downcast nor her eyes uplifted, her head not poked forward, much less hanging down dejectedly, her limbs not lounging but held tense and erect."

These rules are so perfectly horrendous, I would greatly enjoy being in a school or convent where they were enforced – just so that I could rebel, and pay the price.

There is something about strict, unreasonable regimes that makes me squirm. Perhaps, it's that I want to see how long I would last if I tried to outwit the authorities. Or maybe it's that earning punishment is so easy that I would never have to be particularly naughty: simply laughing out loud would be enough.

I like that.

Defiant girl, caned

By Abel on 19 February 2009

A judicial scene played out in my dreams last night, no doubt occasioned by having watched a spanking movie on my laptop in the hotel before falling asleep.

Two girls, newly admitted to the reformatory, stood side-by-side in a cold, whitewashed room – still in the clothes they'd been wearing when sentenced in court. The Governor stood in front of them; another guard watched from the back of the room.

The senior officer gestured towards a large wooden whipping frame in the centre of the room. "You will be aware that all new prisoners receive eight strokes of the cane on admission."

They were.

"Then let's get it over with, shall we? Take off your clothes; the last of you to be naked will receive two extra stripes."

One girl stripped immediately; the other stood with arms folded, not reacting.

He waited until the first girl was naked, then turned to the second: "Did you understand my order, young lady?"

A pause, then a murmured, "Yes."

"Yes, *sir*."

She remained silent.

The governor stepped forward. "Well, if you won't remove your clothes, then we'll have to it for you." He and his colleague moved towards her; one took her wrists, whilst the other stripped her, roughly, as she squirmed to avoid their attentions.

"It seems we have a defiant one here," the senior officer commented to his colleague.

"Indeed, sir."

The governor walked over to the first, more compliant girl. He placed a finger under her chin, and lifted her eyes to his. "It's your lucky day, Miss Hobbs. See, Miss Spencer here clearly needs to be taught a lesson. So I'll be giving her your strokes, as well as her own. Go and stand at the back of the room, facing the wall."

The dream ended there, sadly, before the eighteen strokes (eight for each girl, plus the two for being the last to get undressed) were administered. But later in the night, I slipped back in my dreams to the same reformatory to hear that the girl had just been "put on Section D."

This, it seemed, was shorthand for being sent to the punishment wing for repeated disobedience; whippings would be par for the course. Quite what sections A, B or C were wasn't explained, and my dreams moved on before I could find out more.

The depths of depravity
By Abel on 21 February 2009

I'm talking to Haron in bed about a particular friend, who we've not seen for a while.
"I've never spanked her in private. You know, just me and her."
"Yeah, but you've had sex with her."
"But that wasn't in private, either."
We pause, both contemplating the incident in question. Eventually I break the silence:
"Does it make it more or less pervy that there were four of us in bed at the time?"

The Martyrs' Club
By Abel on 23 February 2009

Sometimes, story plots work themselves out perfectly; sometimes, no matter how much I think about them, the ideas never quite gel. Take a scenario which sprung into my mind early one recent morning, as I walked through Green Park in central London, en route to work.

The headmaster was clearly annoyed: a group of girls had been caned for some serious breach of a school rule. What made it worse was that their crime was a quite calculated gesture: they'd broken a rule widely agreed by the girls in the school to be unfair, and their act had been committed in the full knowledge that it would provoke and annoy the school authorities.

He'd called them in, one by one; each had received a lecture; each had been caned soundly across her skirt and sent on her way.

The grapevine quickly spread word of their punishment around the school, and the girls concerned – far from being ashamed of their punishment – seemed to revel in the attention. That, in their eyes, their canings had been as unfair as the rule they had broken, merely added to their sense of camaraderie, and before long they had styled themselves "The Martyrs' Club."

Posters appeared on noticeboards; slogans scrawled on blackboards; T-shirts were printed and worn under school colours during hockey matches. Their names were whispered by others as a gesture of solidarity and shared defiance: "I support The Martyrs' Club…"

The headmaster had no choice but to act. His lecture at the morning assembly was stern: "I will not stand by and watch a group of girls seek to undermine my authority. Whilst I see no particular need to justify myself to the school, I feel I should point out why the rule in question exists, and why I felt it necessary to administer corporal punishment to the girls in question."

His explanation appeared more than reasonable; the tide of schoolgirl opinion started to turn; he made it clear that their on-going disobedience could not be tolerated, and would be dealt with severely: "Miss Smith, Miss Matthews, Miss Harris, Miss Fry and Miss King will report to my office immediately following this assembly to be caned."

He saw the five girls together this time; called them forward in turn, each to receive six of the very best stripes on the bare. And no more was heard of the Martyrs.

Only, that's where I start to struggle – because I cannot, for the life of me, work out the nature of their original offence. What rule could they have broken, that would seem so manifestly unfair – yet be to eminently reasonable once the rationale for its existence was understood?

Breaking and entering

By Haron on 24 February 2009

I was working on something last night, while in the background the television was on. Through the haze of work I heard snatches of dialogue:
"Yeah, we did have some break-ins. Stole some tools, mindless vandalism, that sort of thing, but..."
The mind completes that sentence without skipping a beat: "But the girls concerned were all apprehended and soundly whipped."
Yes, I'm sure that's *exactly* what went on.

The spanking works of Shakespeare

By Haron on 26 February 2009

On Saturday we went to see the RSC production of Othello. If you disregard the multiple deaths, it was one of the hottest things I've ever seen on the stage.

Patrice Naiambana, who played Othello, had the most wonderful air of power about him, with his voice deep and low, his speech measured. As a general, a figure of authority, he was making my insides melt.

In Act II Scene III his officers had a drunken fight, and Othello walked in to find out what they were up to. (He just happened to be carrying a thin bamboo stick, as well.) His mere presence struck terror into his men, and when he growled "What is the matter, masters?" and "Speak, who began this?", they were quivering like schoolgirls. And so was I, except I wanted to jump up and cry "It was me, sir, I'm so sorry!" He was smoking hot.

When jealousy made him lose his composure and fall into frightening rages, Othello was jumping about the stage with a bull whip, cracking it at Iago, and generally showing he knew how to use it. (He actually used it to strangle Desdemona in the end, but never mind that.) Shame about the jealousy and the whole plot thing, because I was really enjoying the calm, dominant Othello.

That Shakespeare is so kinky, I'm surprised he hasn't been banned.

The secret of the squares
By Abel on 1 March 2009

I love the posher parts of London: those streets of whitewashed Georgian townhouses, far from the madding crowds of shoppers and tourists.

I find the immaculately-maintained private gardens in the middle of the squares particularly enticing. If you've ever strolled around the city, you'll know the sort of place I mean: iron railings, freshly-painted (*always* freshly painted) in black. A locked gate. Inside the railings, a border of trees and thick evergreen foliage – offering a mere glimpse of a footpath inside, around a perfectly-mown lawn in the greenest of greens.

Of course, I'm not posh enough to have ever been inside one of the squares; I'm the sort of hoi polloi that the padlocks are designed to keep out of these most genteel of pastures. But I did stay in a hotel in Belgravia recently facing on to such an oasis – and I finally realised why I find them so fascinating.

Because those trees surrounding the garden, dear readers, were silver birches. And the true purpose of the countless squares suddenly revealed itself. For the daughters of the nobility would need to be kept in order; their maids properly disciplined. And how else would one secure a supply of fresh rods for the administration of city-centre thrashings?

Wrong knickers

By Haron on 7 March 2009

I was dressing for a day out when Abel wandered in and stopped to watch.

I picked out a dress (black with a white floral print), stockings (black), shoes (black) – and suddenly noticed that I was wearing incongruous pink knickers.

"I think I'm wearing wrong colour knickers," I told my watching husband.

"So you are. How dare you wear wrong colour knickers? You need to be caned for that. Bend over."

Huh? What? I gaped at him as he snatched up a cane that was lying on the floor and moved towards me with a look of menace.

"Go on, bend over! Wrong colour knickers are unacceptable!"

I couldn't help giggling as I leaned over the bed. Several quick, sharp slashes fell across my bottom. They stung ferociously, and there seemed to be awfully many of them, although I'm sure there were only five or six. Even through the pain, I laughed like a mad thing. Wrong colour knickers! How dare I!

"I hope that taught you a lesson," said Abel in a savage tone, which was somewhat undermined by a giggle that followed.

"Yessir. Absolutely."

I stood up, rubbing my bottom. And I moved to the cupboard to pick up some correct knickers: black.

I think he just fancied caning me, though.

What the maid saw
By Abel on 13 March 2009

The room was set.

The cords had been tied to the bed – soon to adopt its alternative disguise, as the punishment frame for the reformatory girl who'd been caught absconding.

The cane and tawse had been removed from my bag, and hung in full view on the implement rack (aka lamp), to leave the young woman in no doubt as to her fate.

Only, catching up took priority over playing immediately. My friend and I headed for a drink then dinner.

It was only when we returned and noticed that – in our absence – the bedroom's curtains had been closed and the lamps turned on, that I remembered that the hotel provided an evening turn-down service.

Kink-friendly abode
By Haron on 14 March 2009

This week we've been looking for a new place to live. One estate agent called us back with a description of a house which, he said, was great for our purpose.

"Very cat-friendly," he explained. "It's down a lane, well away from the road."

Abel and I looked at each other, grinning. Down a lane... should be good for our spanking needs. If it had a birch tree nearby, all the better!

The next agent did even better, offering us a flat in a converted school.

These people must know who we are. Or, at least, what we are.

Spring is in the air
By Abel on 15 March 2009

Driving from the north down to London last week, I spied two lambs gambolling in a field beside the motorway. Daffodils are everywhere. Yippee: it feels as though winter's behind us, and the new spring is here.

And you know what that means, don't you?

It's the time of year when Haron starts to tremble. For the birches must be sprouting fresh new shoots: our first forest perambulation of the new season must be drawing close, and with it as a consequence her first birching of the year.

Reformatory girls must have shivered for similar reasons. Birched in February? That's have been with the last of the previous autumn's switches: carefully stored, soaked to bring them back to life, and quite excruciating. Yet compared to a flogging a month or so later, with a birch rod made from fresh, supple, springy switches? I'm supposing that there'd have been a fair few confessions of guilt to the Governor around this time of year, so that matters could be dealt with before the new crop arrived.

Parent-teacher meeting
By Haron on 18 March 2009

A few days ago I found myself in a coffee shop just as it opened at 7.30am.

The only other customers there were an elegant woman in her forties and her teenage daughter. They were silently sipping their coffee and, although they were sitting opposite each other, it was as though there was a concrete wall between them.

I imagined they were about to go to the girl's school. The Headmistress was expecting them.

According to the school's policy, a caning could be administered only in the presence of one of the parents. If this meant that it had to be put off until a convenient date – all the worse for the girl.

The mother would have to sign a witness form, after which her role would be simple: to watch in silent disapproval as her daughter took off her skirt, lowered her knickers and bent over the back of a chair. The punishment wouldn't be unduly harsh, but the girl would remember each of the six burning stripes, as well as the lonely walk to her classroom afterwards.

It would all be finished in time for the mother to get to work by nine: an efficient, clinical execution.

No wonder the pair in the cafe looked so glum.

Public shame

By Haron on 20 March 2009

Today Google has launched its new feature in the UK: Street View, which allows you to type in an address and browse through pictures of street scenes taken in that place.

A representative of Google was talking about this on the breakfast show, when the news person asked him:

There'll be people who say, "I don't want my image on the site, particularly not doing what I was doing in that street on that day."

Too right! Imagine a queue of girls outside the punishment centre on a quiet morning, burning in quiet shame, when a Google camera car snaps a picture of their predicament for all the Internet to see.

And I won't even mention the public floggings, now forever associated with a postcode of an otherwise innocuous town square.

Google has no sympathy towards punished girls.

The headmaster's gramophone
By Abel on 24 March 2009

Needless to say, as we've looked recently for a new place to rent, the question of sound-proofing has been foremost in our minds. Forget the location, the décor, the number of bedrooms – our first assessment on arriving at a potential new home has been of the thickness of the walls. That gorgeous new townhouse, set next to the canal? Far too likely that the neighbours would overhear the sounds of whacking.

I was drawn to picture a headmaster in days gone by. Whilst he'd cane miscreants when strictly necessary, he'd be conscious that the sound of the thrashing would carry through his study's walls and windows. Being a kindly gentleman at heart, he'd hit on a means of saving a girl from having her humiliation relayed to her friends.

Only, you can picture the reaction of a young lady, walking into his room in trepidation – praying that she might escape without a caning – when she saw the headmaster tinkering with the gramophone...

A gothic spanking
By Haron on 25 March 2009

Last night I was home alone, and it was the sort of windy evening that makes glass rattle in the windows and ghosts howl in the chimney. I was warm and cosy indoors, but I imagined that it would be exactly the sort of night when a court-appointed disciplinarian would appear on my doorstep.

I would know he was coming; I would tremble at every rattle and creak of the old house. And yet, when his knock comes, it would be loud and self-assured enough that I could never pretend it was just the rain drumming against my door. My panicking mind would scream at me to not let him inside, but I would rush to open – so that he doesn't get frustrated at standing outside any longer than necessary.

A dark figure against the dark sky, he would hand me the disciplinary notice and confirm my name, and only when I nod would he come in.

He would have a long case – his tools of the trade – and a folding wooden frame. As soon as he walks into the house, he takes complete charge, and nothing I say at this point would delay the pain.

Outside, the wind howls.

A naughty purchase?

By Abel on 28 March 2009

I well recall the feeling of guilt when my younger self ever bought anything, ahem, interesting.

Sneaking into the corner shop to buy 'Men Only' as a teenager (a confusing-titled yet tasteful photographic journal – to be read by men, rather than only featuring men). Blushing, hands shaking, as I handed over my pocket money and stashed the magazine inside my coat.

Some years later, looking nervously around before darting into the Janus shop in Soho. What if someone sees me? They might think I was into naughty things! Help! ("Ten pounds, sir. Nice selection" "Thank you. Not that I'd be reading this myself. It's for a friend.")

Amusingly, similar feelings came to mind the other day, when I was buying... a leather belt. In a perfectly respectable department store. See, I'd forgotten to take one with me on a business trip and I needed one to hold up my jeans.

So there I was, in Marks & Spencer, handing over my selection and parting with the cash... all the time worrying about what the shop assistant must be thinking of me, and blushingly hoping that no-one would notice me making my illicit purchase. (Yes, as it happens, it was the thickest and widest they had on sale. Pure coincidence, I promise you).

Clapping for England

By Haron on 29 March 2009

Yesterday we went to see a game of football at Wembley. Frankly, I was there to look at the stadium, which is really cool, and watch Messrs Beckham and Gerrard being awesome.

But I also got a bonus kinky thrill.

Every spectator got this cleverly folded piece of cardboard, that you're supposed to hold up during the national anthem to make a St George's cross. The name of the thingie? A "clapper banner".

Because, while folded into a cardboard accordion, it's also used to whack really hard on anything you can – your hand, your thigh, an empty seat – it makes a lot of clapping, cheering noise.

Alternatively, you can try to whack it against the bottom of your nearest and dearest, and see what happens.

It proved to be a really lame spanking implement, actually, but it was fun to try.

Thrashed on the train

By Abel on 30 March 2009

Waiting for a train late one recent night on a cold, dark Scottish station, I peered with interest into the ever-so-grand 'Royal Scotsman', occupying the platform opposite mine. Think Orient Express meets Highlands & Islands: a dining room laid with fine china and crystal, elegant drawing rooms, oak-lined corridors leading to snug compartments with armchairs, beds and crisp linens.

Unfortunately, one of the uniformed maids had failed to clean a bathroom mirror with sufficient diligence that morning. For, in one of the train's luxurious bedrooms, she could clearly be seen bending over the arm of a chair, bottom bared. A distinguished-looking gentleman in a dinner jacket was lecturing her sternly.

He removed his thick, black, leather belt. And then, quite properly, he moved to the window and drew the curtains, to spare her from the gaze of the watching crowd.

The fallout
By Haron on 4 April 2009

Last night the news was full of protesters that had been swarming over London. One of the items concerned a girl who had committed criminal damage by throwing a rock at a window of a bank.

The newsreader announced: "She was taken to court today to be given a..."

Abel and I looked at each other and loudly said: "Public flogging."

But it was only a custodial sentence.

For some reason, criminal justice refuses to pander to our twisted imagination.

When there's nobody to help
By Abel on 5 April 2009

Queuing in a Costa Coffee in a student-dominated town the other day, I found myself behind the cutest young lass crying into her boyfriend's arms. He whispered consolation; she broke from her tears to kiss him and smiled, for a brief moment, before the tears returned.

"I'll take care of you," I'm sure he'd said.

"I know you will," she'd doubtless replied. Only she knew, deep down, that he couldn't be there for her when they tied her to the birching bench for the twenty strokes to which the magistrate had just sentenced her.

At least, I think that's what was upsetting her.

Caned before the fireplace

By Abel on 8 April 2009

After a few days away in London, the house was so cold when we returned home last night. I crept into bed first, shivering; Haron came upstairs a few minutes later.

Our conversation turned to a grand country house, on a similarly chill evening. The gentleman owner had been working late in his library; when he found that the fire in his bedroom was unlit – again – he rang for the butler.

"Fetch me the maid and a cane," he instructed. Both appeared within minutes, and the butler was dismissed for the night.

It was little more than two weeks since the previous such incident. "And what did we agree then would happen were there to be a repetition?"

"That you would punish me, sir."

"Indeed. Then light the fire. And then I will honour my word."

He watched her as she arranged the wood. Her hands trembled – whether from the cold, or the fear of the punishment, he knew not. The flames crackled into bright life.

"It appears to be fine now, sir."

"Well. Let's be sure, shall we? You can stand in front of it for five minutes to make sure it's burning well, and once you're confident that it is, I shall cane you."

She was crying by the time he chose to walk across to her, instructing her to touch her toes. He lifted her nightdress, baring her, and picked up the cane. He drew it back high into the air: the six strokes were administered hard, at full strength, each stripe vivid across her pale skin.

Birched in the prison courtyard
By Abel on 10 April 2009

I was struck the other morning by a strange thing about judicial birchings. See, when I imagine or dream or write about these, they always take place either inside, in brightly-lit punishment rooms, or outdoors in the sunshine.

But this particular morning was misty, cold. And suddenly it occurred to me that it was just the sort of morning on which a lass might be led out into the prison courtyard for a birching. It'd be a dark place – overlooked by the barred windows of many of the cells, whose occupants would inevitably hear the punishments taking place down below.

The guard would arrive early at the cell door in question, waking the girls inside. He'd call out a name, and the prisoner would realise that her time had come.

He'd march her down the corridors, lead her outside into the cold morning air, where a small group of official witnesses would be waiting. He'd recite details of the punishment that the court had imposed: that her jail sentence would include a birching, "to be carried out at the convenience of the prison governor".

She'd be ordered to strip – forced to strip, if she resisted – and tied, shivering, to the whipping frame.

And then they'd wait. Wait. Wait. Until the bell of the prison chapel struck seven.

As the echo of its peal faded away, a door to the side of the courtyard would open, and the governor would emerge into the cold. The group would salute.

He'd walk behind the girl. A guard would .read out her details: "Deborah Green. Aged eighteen. Convicted at Wandsworth Crown Court on the fourth of last month on three counts of shoplifting. Sentenced to ten weeks' detention at Her Majesty's pleasure, and thirty strokes of the birch rod."

The governor would hold out his hand, and the first birch would be passed across. He'd pause, measure it, and then commence the flogging...

Painfully bad language

By Haron on 13 April 2009

Yesterday was one of our last sorting-out days before the moving men descend on us. We turned the radio on, opened the front door for ventilation and got to work.

Suddenly, a song came on air that I really didn't approve of. Frustrated, I exclaimed:

"I really hate this fucking song!"

"You hate this *what?*" Abel called back from halfway in a cupboard. "What sort of language is that in the hearing of our neighbours?" He reversed out of the cupboard and said: "Get upstairs."

Oooh, I thought. What fun.

"So sorry, sir," I said, giggling.

We walked into the bedroom together, when Abel said: "All the bloody implements are packed!"

I thought: no shit, sir. But didn't say it.

"This will do," he announced, snatching up my hairbrush and plopping himself on the bed.

Over his knee I went.

The fact that this was all quite funny didn't diminish the atrocious sting of the brush one bit. I yelped and wriggled a lot, but thankfully, it was over soon. He let me up, put down the brush and started to walk away.

I rubbed my bottom.

"That really fucking hurt," I said petulantly.

"It *what?*"

He spun on his heel, and marched right back, picking up the hairbrush on the way.

Of course, Abel has the filthiest mouth known to humankind, which is why whenever he tries to spank me for swearing, it can't be anything other than in fun.

It still hurt, though.

I probably didn't swear again for a whole *hour*.

Moving, breaking in

By Abel on 14 April 2009

So, we're almost ready to move to our new home. Our belongings are suitably de-kinked: three large sealed crates bear the more pervy of our books; the implements are carefully stashed in a pair of hockey bags and a tightly-taped poster tube.

The long box marked (and full of) "School Canes" lies ready to be transported in my car – deemed too shocking to leave for the guys moving our belongings. So too is our other wooden box – the one containing the tawse, bible and rosary beads, its lid inscribed with a cross and the well-worn words "Holy Trinity Roman Catholic School for Girls. Discipline Records and Correctional Procedure Guidelines". I may have a fair collection of literature on the, ahem, history of education on the bookshelves for the team to pack, but if they're religious types, they might not be impressed with our favourite scholastic artefact. (Actually, even if they're *not* religious types, they might not be impressed!).

The whole thing's very exciting – not least, the thought of our first evening in the new place. See, the truck with our stuff won't arrive until the morning after we move in – and the place we're renting is unfurnished. Our first night will therefore be spent in a near-empty house – sleeping on an inflatable bed, accompanied by one small suitcase, the boxes of implements that I've transported, and not much else.

I shall be the property agent, we've decided, responding to reports that a squatter's been seen inside the supposedly-empty house. I shall catch Haron red-handed, although she may well try to hide. (Hey, it'll be a good way to explore!).

She won't want to be taken to the police for breaking in; a sound caning is sure to follow. I'm sure it won't be the last night she'll spend sleeping, striped, on her front in our new home!

Here, unpack the canes

By Haron on 17 April 2009

Abel's parents phoned a few nights ago, very apologetic for not having offered to come and help us unpack in our new home.

Why yes, it would have been a grand idea. Given what we suspect about Abel's father, I'm sure he would enjoy unboxing the five crates of dubious books. When he was done, he could help us find a home for all the toys, magazines, videos and pictures.

Or maybe they should just stay well away until we designate a kinky zone, which can be safely locked on any future visits.

It's actually a cane

By Haron on 21 April 2009

I never fail to be amused by how sellers of spanking toys describe their products on customs declarations.

Say, today we got a box in the post.

It contained, according to the notice, "a wand".

I didn't remember buying any Harry Potter merchandise...

"Your First Headship"

By Abel on 22 April 2009

I came across a long-forgotten book during our packing, entitled "Your First Headship". We picked it up years ago in a second-hand bookshop, wondering what it said about disciplinary matters.

Sadly, it was rather lacking in useful advice. But I did find myself mentally re-writing it along the following lines the other day during a long drive:

> Corporal Punishment
>
> It is imperative that, in your early days as a headmaster, you make it plain to the girls in the school that you will resort to corporal punishment to punish those committing more serious misdemeanours.
>
> We recommend that you make an example of one of the girls within the first two weeks of your Headship. Ideally, you will find a 'good girl', not one typically badly-behaved, who has overstepped the mark.

Announce your displeasure at her offence in school assembly, and tell her to report to your office at morning break. By making the fact of her punishment public, you will send out a clear and important message.

Keep her waiting for a few minutes, then scold her severely and express your disappointment. Administer the caning hard – six of your very best with the senior cane, on the bare, with her touching her toes. Have no doubt that news of the procedure that you follow will be disseminated across the school within a matter of hours, just as her stripes will be inspected in the changing room showers in days to come for signs of your effectiveness as a disciplinarian.

By being strict in these early days, you will be kinder to the girls in the longer-term, making it clear that misbehaviour will be soundly punished, and thus reducing the incidence of rule-breaking and the need to administer future canings.

The St. George's Day birchings
By Abel on 23 April 2009

Today, of course, is St. George's Day. Sadly, England is rather lax at celebrating its patron saint's day – other than the occasional promotion of cheap beer in the pubs. Me? I'd have flags flying everywhere, and a public holiday.

Still, I'm reminded that, not too many years ago, the date was marked in girls' reformatories across England – albeit perhaps not in a manner that would be deemed entirely celebratory. Picture the scene: it's after breakfast (water, dry bread) in the reformatory on 23rd April. The girls are gathered together around the walls of the main hall. In the centre of the room, the whipping block. A birch rod rests on top.

The governor strides in, and takes a piece of paper from his pocket. He opens it, slowly, reads the name to himself, looks round the room.

"Sarah Fisher, step forward."

She's pushed to the front of the crowd; finds herself face-to-face with the Governor. He looks over her, at the assembled girls. "You will know, of course, of the St. George's Day Birching. How our Prime Minister, Mr. Gladstone, outlawed the use of corporal punishment in the girls' judicial system. How his eminent opponent, Mr. Disraeli, forced a late amendment to the bill before parliament. 'Without fear of the sanction of the birch, I fear that girls may run riot.'"

As a result, he continued, once a year the Governor was obliged by law to select the girl whose behaviour in the previous twelve months had fallen furthest short of the expected standards. And to punish her. In public, before the other inmates.

"Miss Fisher: remove your dress, and bend over the punishment bench."

"Please, sir. There must be a mistake."

"When it comes to the governance of this institution, girl, I don't make mistakes." And he'd proceed to tie the naked lass in position – buckling the leather straps tightly around her wrists and her ankles.

The birching would be severe – a once-in-a-year lesson to the assembled crowd on the need to behave. For, after all, one of them (averting their eyes, peeking at the flogging in fascinated terror) could find herself there next year, howling as the rod cut home, sharply, repeatedly, until the Governor was satisfied that the girl's chastisement had sent out an appropriate message.

Anyone for tennis?

By Abel on 24 April 2009

Staying with Cath at the moment; the discussion yesterday morning turned to tennis skirts. Perhaps inevitably, during the day I corrupted the images of cute girls in their tennis whites into a rather interesting scene.

The school's tennis team was good: one of the best in the country. They'd travelled for miles for the final of an inter-school competition; their opponents had put them up for a night in a spare dormitory.

Rather than going to bed early to prepare for their big day, however, the six young ladies stayed up late. They were caught by one of the prefects of their host school, at two in the morning, singing merrily – a result, no doubt, of the bottles of vodka now empty and littering the dorm.

News would filter back the following morning to their master, who would address them sternly in the changing room before the tournament. "I know what happened last night: your duty to your school is to demonstrate today that your misbehaviour won't compromise your performance on the courts."

Only, of course, it did, as they crashed to a spectacular defeat – losing every match. The girls stood, heads bowed, as their opponents were presented with the prestigious trophy, and then turned disconsolate to troop back to the dressing room.

"Not so fast. Out onto the court, now. And line up facing the net."

He'd walk behind them, lecturing. "I'm ashamed of you all for disgracing the good name of the school. As is the headmaster, to whom I spoke this morning, and who has asked me to punish you."

He'd turn and beckon to the head prefect from the host school, who'd walk onto court carrying a cane borrowed from one of the housemasters. Skirts and underwear would be removed; the girls would be instructed to bend over, legs straight, and touch the court in front of their toes. He'd start at one end of the line, swishing the cane through the air to get used to its weight and balance. And then he'd administer six hard strokes to the first of the culprits, before moving along to stripe her neighbour.

The third girl would be the captain of tennis – and a school prefect, no less. The master would pass by: "I'll deal with you in a moment." The three girls to her right would each take their six strokes – yelping, clutching their backsides, hoping their friends wouldn't notice the tears. And then he'd return to the captain.

"Had you done your duty, none of this would have happened – and none of your friends would have been caned. You'll receive double."

Twelve of the very best later, the girls were ordered to stand and dress. "Shower* and get changed quickly. I want to see you at the minibus in fifteen minutes' time." And the master would beckon their host's head prefect, who'd been watching with interest from the side of the court, and hand back the cane.

–

Interestingly, when we played the scene in the evening, it wasn't the on-court canings that were re-enacted. Rather, the tennis captain was called into the headmaster's study on her return to the school.

He expressed his considerable disappointment: "And whilst you have already been punished as captain of tennis, it falls to me to deal with the disgrace you have brought on the office of prefect. I expect far higher standards than this." And another sound caning followed...

Left inside, alone

By Haron on 25 April 2009

I could have a massive sulk now. Today I was supposed to be with a group of my spanking girlfriends for a girls' weekend away, but at the last moment I got derailed by flu, and had to stay at home, in bed.

I don't like sulking, though. Instead, I'm turning this into a fantasy: I'm a daughter of a big 18th century family, and all of us had been invited to a neighbouring estate to a big gathering. The adults would hunt and dance, and we young people would do young people things.

Except the night before the event, my governess complained to my mother that I'd been making a fuss about the dress I'm supposed to wear. Mother told Papa, and he swiftly dispensed judgement: if I'm not grateful for the treats I get, I shan't get any treats at all.

The family has left. My governess and I remain. Instead of picnics with my friends, I get to sit in additional lessons, practise my embroidery and go to bed early. And each night before bed, the governess has the order to put me over her lap, pull up my white nightgown, and spank me with an ebony hairbrush until I'm tearful and repentant.

Papa has promised that, upon his return, he will interview me in his study, and if he doesn't find my attitude changed, he will send a footman to cut a birch, and administer the punishment personally.

The weekend is dull with none of my siblings here, but I dread its end.

A painful awakening
By Haron on 1 May 2009

A couple of days ago I was quietly working at my desk. Very quietly, in fact; anybody in the same room might have thought I was asleep.

Abel walked in and, seeing me with my head on the desk and my eyes closed, made the same conclusion. "Upstairs, young lady!" he commanded, waking, er, distracting me from work.

Despite the imminent threat of punishment, I couldn't help giggling as I followed him to his study. He lectured me about work habits, but I could do nothing but giggle.

"This is not a laughing matter!" Abel said, brandishing a cane. "Trousers down. Touch your toes."

I did, biting on a smile. He delivered six strokes, not the hardest ever, but stinging and quite impressive.

"Do you still think it's funny?" he asked.

Oh, dear... It was! But could I admit that being found snoozing at my desk was pretty funny, whether or not it was also painful?

"A little bit," I suggested as a compromise.

Abel didn't like it at all. "Bend over!" he ordered.

Ouch. Six more strokes, harder this time, in quick succession. I yelped and wriggled a lot.

"Let this be a lesson for you," said Abel. "Go back to work, young lady."

Luckily, he didn't ask whether I still found it funny.

Because, well...

OTK vs. OTF
By Abel on 2 May 2009

I found myself reflecting the other day on the relative merits of giving a spanking OTK (over the knee, as most kinky types will know) and OTF – over the furniture.

See, my spanko interests originated in the world of school fantasies. And, in those, it would have been quite unacceptable for there to be any physical contact between master and pupil. Bending over a desk or the back of a wooden chair were thus the oft-imagined punishment positions in my emerging kinky reveries. There were occasional diversions to the arm of a solid leather sofa in the headmaster's office, or to the end of a dormitory bed. But spanking – or more specifically caning – was very much an OTF affair.

The only exception was bending over... well, over nothing, as some girls found themselves touching their toes. And as my kink developed, and the schools morphed into castles and prisons, whipping benches appeared on my scene – still with the girl at the end of a cane or birch. That one could collect such a variety of implements added to the attraction.

And then I started spanking more folks for real, and found the women with whom I was playing draping themselves over my lap. What on earth? From a role-play perspective, I rather struggled: my schoolmasters still couldn't bring themselves to touch their naughty charges, and as for fatherly spankings... well, uncles or guardians were as far as I could comfortably go. But even then, I was more likely to unbuckle my belt.

Then, of course, my playmates started to misbehave, getting themselves into trouble – and I found that real-life misdemeanours requiring punishment lent themselves more naturally to instructing a girl to assume the position across my lap. And the fact that a good, firm hand spanking could make a lass writhe so (and trust me, my hand spankings are usually pretty firm) meant that the absence of an implement wasn't a problem. Fingers could even leave marks, just like a cane stroke!

At this point, I rather blush. For, of course, spanking at this point can (with the right and willing partner) take on a more overtly naughty dimension. Hands might stroke and caress, to comfort a girl's sore behind – and they might tend to stray. But god forbid that she would sense any, erm, rising interest on my part as she lay draped across me. (Shy, me, see!)

So now I find I can enjoy both, in almost equal but quite different measures. My deep-down loyalty lies with positioning a girl OTF, but the attractions of OTK do rather appeal. I'm still left with struggling to reconcile the idea of combining the two, though – for me, it needs to be either OTT *or* OTF, and combining them feels somehow wrong. Warm-ups before (say) a caning are therefore a challenge – I can never quite mentally justify how to integrate them into a formal punishment scene.

And then, of course, there's TTAB (Tied To A Beam), but that's another story…

Whipped across the room
By Haron on 3 May 2009

I am now a very proud and pleased owner of a swivelly desk chair. It's large and comfy, with convenient little wheels on its feet.

Abel and I rolled it into the house this morning, paused in the middle of the room and looked at each other.

"Do the wheels lock?" Abel asked.

"Um, no."

"So," he said, "what would happen if you were whipping a girl on it?"

"I don't know," I said, grinning at the mental picture. "She would swivel round and round."

"No," he said. "She would travel along the room with each stroke. You could say to a girl, *'I will whip you across the room.'* And continue the whipping until she reached the opposite wall."

I really don't know about that: it would take an awfully hard stroke, I think, to shift a chair with a girl along the carpet. I'm curious whether this would work, but I'm not keen to test the theory on my own bottom.

Any volunteers, perhaps?

Norwegian wood

By Abel on 9 May 2009

Norway's expensive, right? Everyone knows that. Yet I was still taken aback at the price of dinner in Stavanger earlier this week. Cheese omelette with small green salad, apple pie, small bottle of beer. Guess how much?

Forty pounds.

Forty!

Admittedly, I was staying in a lovely little seaside hotel, carefully restored and filled with antique furniture over which generations of Norwegian daughters and maids had doubtless been bent to be whipped. But forty pounds? (Thank goodness I didn't go for the cod and chips – that was £38 on its own!)

It was a pleasant surprise, therefore, when I discovered that the following morning's (quite excellent) breakfast buffet was included in the room rate. And my mind started drifting... See, they trusted their guests: I wasn't even asked for my room number.

Picture, then, four local girls – best friends, traipsing every morning in the wind and the rain along the desolate coastal road. They'd stare in at the hotel guests – warm, well-fed, in the lap of some luxury – as they walked past towards their school.

"What if we went in one morning?"

And so the plot was hatched. They left their homes half an hour early. Wore casual jumpers over their school uniform dresses. Walked into the hotel, treated themselves to breakfast, and left – elated, and completely unchallenged.

The knock on their classroom door came late in the morning: a senior girl entered, bearing a note. Their form master read it, folded it away, then looked up. "It appears that four of you are in rather a lot of trouble. Would the following put their books away, and report to the headmaster's study." Their hearts were pounding by now: they scarcely needed him to read their names to *know*...

The hotel staff would have realised that the four were impostors, and their dresses would have identified them as girls from the local school. Their descriptions would have been written down; that they were the same girls who walked past the manager's window every morning would not have escaped notice. Identification, once he had been shown in to see the Head, would have been the simplest of tasks.

But I'm far from certain how they'd have been punished. Would they have been brought before the headmaster en masse and birched in turn? Would he have had them sent in one-by-one, punishing a girl then sending her to stand facing the wall (bare, red bottom on display) whilst he called in the next lass for her thrashing... (And would the hotel manager have been invited to stay to witness their correction?)

Or would the Head's lecture note the gravity of the offence – a letter home (leading to inevitable excruciating consequences that evening) preceding a public birching before the whole school in the following morning's assembly?

The tawse of nightmares
By Haron on 11 May 2009

There must be a law that, if you live in a new place, you must fill it with new stuff. That's what Abel has been doing since we moved: he's gone on an implement shopping spree.

The latest arrival has been a replica ROSLA* tawse. It's a handsome artefact: greyish-white, quite short (travel size, Abel said gleefully), and, alas, as thick as three stacked pound coins. Ouch.

The day it arrived we had both been quite busy, so I undressed for bed and slipped under the covers without a single worried thought. A few minutes later, Abel arrived – and he was carrying the new tawse.

"What sort of behaviour do you call this, young lady?" he asked. "Kneel on the bed, you're going to get punished."

Right. Apparently, I was a bad girl. Oh, well.

Our bed is also new, and we're still experimenting with the positions that may or may not work with it. This time, I was on hands and knees across the bed, feet dangling over the edge. It was quite comfortable, and gave Abel plenty of safe swinging room, which I had cause to regret right away.

"I'm really sorry, sir," I said, despite not having anything to be sorry for. It just seemed like the right thing to say, when there's a man behind you with a big old tawse.

Not that it worked. Abel swung, and thwacked the tawse across my bottom. He didn't use very much force, but the pain was disproportionate, both deep and fiery, and I had cause to worry that it would only get worse from here. Which was, of course, right: having measured my reaction, he felt comfortable going harder. Not even a lot harder, but I felt it, and howled like a disgruntled ghost.

I had real trouble staying in position, and with each stroke was crawling further and further away from the edge. This didn't impress Abel, who had to order me to stick my bottom out in an increasingly firm tone of voice. It took an awesome burst of willpower to stay put for the final, sixth stroke, which was, traditionally the hardest, and burned infernally.

I know very well that Abel didn't use the tawse with anything approaching real strength, and it's pretty much the only way I would ever play with it again: the thing is evil. A few of our hardier friends may enjoy its full range of pain, though, so I'm glad to have it in our arsenal.

Plus, it's pretty.

* ROSLA, for those of you not obsessed with British school history, is Raising of School Leaving Age – government acts that extended the length of compulsory schooling. Last time this was done, the teachers worried that the tawses they were using wouldn't be effective on older pupils, and so a range of thicker, more horrible tawses was introduced to impress them. Personally, I'm still quite impressed with normal tawses at the age of 29, so I think they might not have bothered...

Stealing the banned books
By Abel on 16 May 2009

I read a review recently of an intriguing-sounding book, "The Forbidden Best-Sellers of Pre-Revolutionary France", by Professor Robert Darnton of Princeton

University. Sadly, the books concerned seem to have been more political than erotic – but the review still included an interesting line:

> It was the public hangman's duty to destroy forbidden books that had been confiscated, but fortunately for historians he frequently did not, choosing instead to lacerate and burn dummy copies while the magistrates kept the originals.

I'd picture it a little differently. The magistrates would hand the banned books to the hangman for disposal. So they'd be puzzled – and furious – when several of the confiscated tomes were brought before them once again and found, on close inspection, to be the very same copies they'd previously sent for destruction.

The hangman would deny any knowledge of how this might have happened; it was only when a warrant was issued for his arrest that his daughter and maidservant would confess their dastardly scheme. For they were the ones who'd swapped the outlawed volumes for perfectly-innocent novels, and taken handsome sums from the booksellers for their illicit wares.

The magistrates would be unanimous in their sentence: the young women would be taken in chains to the marketplace, where they'd receive the soundest of public floggings, one girl after the other. I rather suspect that the hangman himself might have been the one wielding the birch...

The escape committee

By Abel on 16 May 2009

Sometimes, I think spanking stories are best cut off early, leaving the subsequent detail to the reader's imagination. I've been playing with the following, for example, for a while now – tweaking words here and there on my laptop in idle moments.

I personally think it works better than if I'd kept writing and described the whole flogging. I wonder if readers agree?

"I am prepared to be lenient", the Governor explained.

The line of uniformed girls looked at him, looked at the whip in his hand, looked at their friend at the end of the hall – naked, her hands tied above her head, the rope thrown over a beam lifting her to her tiptoes. Lenient?

"Regulation 23.4: 'any prisoner associated with an attempt to plan an escape shall be flogged'. You were all party to the conversation that Officer Lucas overheard in the refectory: that is more than enough evidence."

Each girl, contemplating a protest. Thinking better of it; remaining silent.

He continued. "Prisoner 8974 here was sitting at the head of the table. I shall therefore deem her responsible for your plot. And you may trust that I shall not be as lenient with her. Nor with any of you, should you disobey an order at any future point in your sentence."

The Governor walked behind her, tall and powerful next to her slight, pale frame. "Twenty lashes. The rest of you shall watch carefully, and learn the consequences..."

He drew back the whip, with an expert hand, and cracked it down hard. Its leather tongues fanned out, kissing her like serpents. Her scream filled the chamber, echoing from the rafters.

He took her face in his gloved hand, and lifted her eyes to meet his. "Regretting your conspiracy already, my dear? And I've scarcely started..."

So much left unstated. Did he whip her across the buttocks, or the back? Did the lashes stripe her bare breasts? Did she maintain a degree of bravery, or succumb abjectly to the anguish of her whipping?

Did she take the whole punishment on behalf of the group, or (in her anguish) betray the real leader of their escape plan in the hope of mercy? And if she did, how did the Governor react? (I rather suspect he would have completed her twenty lashes, before punishing the other girl too).

And what of those watching? Perhaps the Governor caught one of them looking away: would she too be brought to the front, stripped and flogged in turn?

Parental consent

By Haron on 20 May 2009

A couple of days ago we witnessed an interesting scene at a train station. Two young ladies attempted to go through the ticket barrier using "child" tickets, and were challenged by the ticket inspector.

"We're 15!" they assured him in chorus.

I shared his obvious mistrust. I wouldn't have been surprised to see those girls on a university campus; they may have belonged at school, just, but children they were not.

The inspector was sceptical. "What if I called your parents?" he asked. "What would they say?"

The girls assured him that their parents would confirm the story. Although the inspector didn't look at all convinced, he let them through in the end – they were, perhaps, more trouble than they were worth, and there was a queue building up.

I imagined a different outcome. The inspector would buzz for a colleague to watch the gate, and would take the two girls to the station office. From there, he would call their respective parents. Dejectedly, the girls would listen to his side of the conversation. "I see. Yes, I thought seventeen was a more likely age... The fine is £50. Of course, they can wait here until you bring the money. Hmm, that's an interesting alternative, sir; I agree, very fitting."

He would thrust the phone at one of them: "Your father wants a word."

The negotiations wouldn't take very long: both fathers would be in agreement that a sound whipping would benefit the two girls, and the ticket inspector would agree to do the deed and to waive the fine.

With the door of the office locked, he would make them take turns bending over the small desk. His uniform belt would make a most effective implement, slicing through the air, cracking against unprotected skin. The girls would do their best to keep their cries from reaching the busy station on the other side of the door.

...Or perhaps, the story would be completely different: upon reaching the girls' parents on the phone, the inspector would find out that they were, indeed, fifteen years old. He would apologise and let them go. But at home, they would have to face their irate fathers. "Have I not told you before to dress your age? What's this on your face, make-up? Go to your room, young lady, and wait for me in the corner."

You know you're a pervert when...
By Abel on 23 May 2009

... your business meetings in Amsterdam finish early, you go for a walk, and all the sex shops seem *so* tame! Not a decent implement in sight.

I had to compensate with a visit to the Torture Museum ("The procedures of Inquisition, shameful and corporal punishments... Learn the painful truth..."). That too was rather dull – not a whip in sight, although some of the illustrations were rather nice. Sorry, rather shocking and scary.

But it was the coffee shop that I passed later which sparked interesting ideas – 'coffee' in this context being more (legal) cannabis than cappuccino. I pictured a schoolmaster in the hotel reception, in a state of some agitation – his 'lights out' room-by-room roll call having determined that two of the young ladies in his care had failed to return that evening.

They'd show up before long – just as he was debating whether to call the police to report them missing. The pair would be skimpily-dressed, overly-made-up, unstable on their feet and incredibly giggly.

"We've been for a *coffee*, sir. A legal one." (Snigger). "We forgot the time. But you're nice, sir, and we knew you wouldn't mind..."

But mind he did, and their demeanour back at school a few days later would be rather different as they stood before the headmaster. Six strokes each on the bare would precede a one-week suspension; they'd touch their toes side-by-side for their caning, before being sent to pack and await the arrival of their respective fathers to take them to their homes...

Traditional values

By Haron on 25 May 2009

Yesterday, there was a sound spanking occurring in our bedroom (not of me, but I was present, along with a small group of spectators). The hairbrush was making the awesome cracking sounds you expect when a wooden surface connects with a bare bottom. There were some squeaks and yelps coming from the spanked girl.

When we came downstairs afterwards, we found that, while all of this was going on in a room just above the front door, we'd been left a leaflet by the Conservative Party.

How very, very appropriate. And what a shame that a canvasser didn't actually knock on the door: we could have demonstrated that the conservative values are alive and well in the region. In a manner of speaking.

A subtle invitation
By Haron on 31 May 2009

This morning I was supervising the warming of milk in the microwave. This involved bending over at the waist, so that I could see what was happening in there.

Abel walked past. Stopped. Looked at me. (I saw him reflected in the glass door of the microwave). "Hmm," he said, and casually lifted the hem of my morning dress. "Stay there."

The thing about milk is that you absolutely cannot leave it unsupervised, otherwise it will explode out of its mug and try to take over the kitchen. Even if I was tempted to flee, I was effectively tied to the domestic appliance, like a 1950s wife.

I watched in the glass as Abel went to the next room and picked up a branch of pussy willow out of a big floor vase. He moved towards me with menace in his step, and gave me a hard slash across the bottom.

"Owww!" I said, and then said something rude. And then my milk started boiling, so I scrambled to subdue it.

Abel quietly examined my bottom in search of a mark. "It's right there!" I said, pointing at a spot that felt like somebody sliced it with a knife.

"No mark," said Abel sulkily. "Obviously, it wasn't hard enough. There're bits of pussy willow all over the kitchen, young lady; pick them up."

I stuck out my lower lip, commenting that bending over in this house was some sort of magical cue for people to appear behind you with implements.

Abel asked whether I wished to tell him that I hadn't bent over with exactly that purpose in mind.

Ah. Well. If you put it like that...

The girl in the pub
By Abel on 7 June 2009

One really couldn't help but notice the lass over by the bar in our favourite local pub last night – gorgeously pretty, in a figure-hugging black dress. I speculated: why was she waiting alone, toying with her half-pint of lemonade, glancing at her phone every few seconds, willing it to ring?

Ah, I worked out: she was waiting for her boyfriend. See, it was the leavers' ball at the local public school. And he'd invited her, of course. He was due here any moment to pick her up and take her to the celebration.

Only, she'd been a pupil in the same year at the same school. Until last summer, when she'd been caught breaking some sacrosanct school rule. Caned by her housemaster. Expelled by the headmaster.

This would be the first time she'd been back since. She'd be amongst old friends, of course; many would have stayed in touch. But the staff would be there, too. And simply walking through the school gates would bring back so many memories – not least, of the last time she'd walked *out* of them on that fateful day a year ago.

(She was actually presumably just going out for the night. But I thought my version was better. And when I remembered that the poshest school locally is all-girls, and realised that it would therefore have been her *girlfriend* taking her to the ball, the whole thing seemed almost too perfect not to be true!)

Living with her choices
By Haron on 8 June 2009

Strolling across a sunny village green last week, we observed a family having a picnic. The daughter, a girl of about seventeen, had short, hot pink hair.

"Hmm," said Abel. "Nice of her parents to let her keep the colour after they'd spanked her for dying her hair in the first place."

Me, I imagined a different story.

Once the spanking was over, and she stood in the corner with her jeans down, hands itching – but not daring – to fall to her smarting red bottom and give it a sneaky rub – her father asked if she'd learned her lesson.

"I have, I promise," she said, sniffling between words. "It's a silly colour, I don't know what possessed me. I'll have it re-dyed tomorrow."

"Oh, no, young lady," said her father. "You will keep the colour for two weeks, so that everyone can see what a silly girl you were. Learn to live with the consequences of your rash decisions."

Her spanking may have been over... but her punishment was not.

The guardian's back-story
By Abel on 9 June 2009

Girls in my stories and scenes often end up being dealt with by their guardian. It's a convenient role – domestic rather than scholastic, but avoiding the need for parental punishment (such things relatively rarely being my thing).

The arrangements vary, but usually the girl's parents are no longer on the scene (some unspoken tragedy having befallen them several years before). The guardian is usually wealthy, always lives in a big house, is single and childless. The girl will be at boarding school; she'll return to his house for school holidays. He'll be caring – but somewhat aloof, and uncompromisingly strict.

It struck me the other morning, though, thinking about a future scene, that such figures are usually fairly two-dimensional in my kinky reveries. So I set about dreaming up more on my guardian character.

See, he'd grown up in the same street as the girl's mother. They'd been best friends – even when the boys usually played with boys, and the girls with the girls, and never the twain did meet. Only children; their parents close; both of their houses almost equally home to each of them.

They'd explored the world with each other and through each other's experiences. They'd confided, commiserated and comforted when needed. They'd cuddled – but chastely; they were too close for friendship to turn into a 'relationship'; more brother-and-sister than boyfriend-and-girlfriend.

And then they'd gone to different universities, and she'd met a charming young man, and before too long she'd graduated, married – their daughter arriving a year or so later. The choice of godfather was an easy and obvious one; he'd been honoured and delighted.

He'd watched the girl grow up into a striking and successful young woman – so like her mother at that age. (And, before you wonder, as with her mother, his thoughts were entirely proper!).

Her parents had been posted overseas when she was 15, and a scholarship pupil at the most prestigious girls' boarding school. (I like the idea of 'posted', rather than some disastrous accident!). And they'd asked whether he would be her guardian. (It wouldn't be feasible for her to visit them, for some reason. I know: they were anthropologists living for an extended period deep in the jungle!).

So the girl moved into one of the spare rooms in his house; stayed with him in the vacations – even been taken with him across Europe every summer to broaden her cultural education, staying in grand hotels. He took great pride in her success at school – which he documented in long, hand-written letters to her parents, which reached them weeks later.

And the use of corporal punishment – after all, the starting point for my scenario? Very infrequent; *in loco parentis*, as they had requested. But used, nonetheless, even as he remembered consoling her mother years before as she cried into his shoulder – after those rare occasions on which she'd been sent to bend over the dining table or the end of her bed, for a whipping with a doubled-over belt. Only, as a gentleman, he preferred to use the cane – when strictly necessary.

A long walk uphill

By Haron on 10 June 2009

Last week, chasing a patch of sunshine, we went for a drive into the countryside. On the edge of a picturesque Cotswolds village I looked along a narrow side road to see it run up a steep hill, near the summit of which there perched a lone house.

That, I realised, was where the local disciplinarian used to live. If I were a local girl, my misbehaviour would normally be dealt with by my father. But if he thought I was being particularly obstinate, he could send me to walk up the hill, so that I could explain myself to That Man In The House.

He would receive me in a room specially equipped for dealing with local delinquents. I would try very hard not to look at the array of implements displayed on the wall, or the various stools and benches in a row. My sins being relatively small, all he would need would be a straight-backed chair and an ebony hairbrush – not unlike what I would expect at home, but so much more frightening in the hands of That Man.

Unlike my father, he would have no qualms about spanking me until I cried and hung limply over his lap. He would explain that, when I grew older, if I didn't mend my ways, he would punish me much worse – would I care to take a look at his canes and straps?

I would shake my head, eyes shut tights, and promise that I would never, ever be naughty again.

We would both know that eventually I would be back.

Borrowed authority

By Haron on 14 June 2009

My dream landscape has righted itself again, serving up a lovely, though brief, dream of a girl punished by her older brother. She was still at school, whereas he nobly came home from college to watch her for a few weeks while their parents were on holiday.

The part that I dreamed of was where she challenged him: you can't spank me! You're not a grown-up! And in response he offered her a phone, and asked whether she'd like to call their dad and ask him about it.

She very, very quickly decided that a spanking from her brother would be preferable to that particular discussion.

In the morning I realised that in all my vast role-playing career I've never once played a brother/sister scene. Initially, this would have been because I didn't know any tops close enough to me in age for this to work. Now I do, though, so maybe I should see what I can initiate...

Took myself out to the ball game

By Abel on 15 June 2009

By the time this pops up on the blog, I'll be half-way across the Atlantic, coming home after my conference. I can't wait to be back – to cuddle Haron, to meet up with the big group of spanko friends who are coming for dinner on Tuesday night, to be able to have long conversations without worrying that the mobile phone is costing me £1.35 per minute...

I stayed over at the resort for a couple of days once the event had finished, given that the international flights cost £1000 less if the stay included a Saturday night. And, with time to kill, I took a few of my team out to the local baseball stadium to watch a game. It was a great evening out – beer, hot dogs, popcorn (and even a game to watch, not that I know the rules).

One feature of the stadium was a huge, huge video screen. Alongside a wealth of information about the players were pictures of people in the crowd, and messages sent from one fan to another.

The two might be combined, I speculated. A father, out with business colleagues, would see a photograph of his daughter and her friends – in the stadium, playing truant. The note would appear on the screen a few moments later: "Jessica in block 309. You should be at school. Go straight to your room when you get home. I'll deal with you when I get back. Love from Daddy."

Or maybe he'd summon her to his executive suite; the next time the camera roamed around the crowd, it would focus in on the young lady over her father's knee – shorts and panties down as he spanked her. Each swat would be cheered by the 30,000-strong crowd, her reddening bottom filling the screen and quite distracting the players...

Self-inflicted punishment
By Haron on 18 June 2009

That's my punishment I'm talking about – it was entirely self-inflicted, and I'm not talking about self-flagellation here.

A few days ago I drove to see some friends, an hour and a bit each way. I got there fine. I got back fine.

I might have driven a bit... fast. The motorway was moving at well above the speed limit, and I decided it was safer to go with the flow than putter along at 70 behind a cement mixer, letting everyone in the world overtake me.

After Abel came back from the US, I expressed to him the surprise that everyone drove so fast here in the South, and admitted that I felt a little naughty for having followed the crowd.

It was immediately clear that he didn't feel I was only "a little" naughty. In a very dangerous voice, he ordered me to go straight upstairs, to his study.

I must say that I wasn't terribly disappointed at this turn of events, because hey, we'd been apart for a week, and there's nothing like a spanking to bring you closer together. Still, I might have liked it better if he hadn't reached straight for a massive frat paddle of doom.

That paddle? It hurts. I got five swats, all uniformly crisp and burning through the seat of my jeans. I might have howled a bit, and I definitely jumped up in a very undignified manner – but it *hurt*! I don't usually strive for dignity under such circumstances.

Still, I can't help thinking that the whole thing was my own silly fault for mentioning it to Abel in the first place. It's not like there's speed traps on the motorway, or anything. He would have never *known*.

The first-year examination
By Abel on 19 June 2009

Come with me to a rather unusual establishment: an exclusive University campus, for the country's very brightest girls. Only a small number are accepted – fifty per year, perhaps, hand-picked after careful scrutiny of those recommended in confidential letters from their schools. They're guaranteed high-flying jobs in the State administration when they leave – this being a country where the State controls everything.

The place is run along boarding school lines: uniforms, strict rules, girls required to remain on campus at all times during the term. There's the ever-present (but rarely-used) threat of the cane for those who underperform.

It's the end-of-year examination for the first year students. The exam takes place over three days: three papers per day, each incredibly testing. Each paper can pose questions on any of the topics studied during the year.

Exactly 48 hours after the final paper is completed, a league table of results will be published on the University noticeboard – a percentage score against each girl's name, with the top student at the head of the list. And, to focus them on their studies throughout their first year, there's a long-standing tradition that whoever finishes bottom of the class will be caned.* Twelve strokes on the bare, in front of her peers – the only time a punishment is ever given in public.

We're in the exam room. It's the morning of day two. The students are writing away, feverishly. The invigilator roams from desk to desk. Something catches his eye across the room – a girl behaving strangely. He walks on, closer, behind the girl in question, observing without being observed. Closer still, and his suspicions are confirmed.

Suddenly he's next to her, taking the wooden ruler from her desk, turning it over and seeing (as he'd suspected) tiny hand-written notes: formulae, dates, names. He breaks the silence: "Stand up and explain yourself!"

She rises to her feet, but can only offer a mumbled excuse: "I...I used it for revising, sir. I didn't mean to bring it into the exam with me."

"Sit down and continue your work," he tells her. "You'll keep working on this and the other papers, as usual. But be in no doubt that you will be accorded a score of zero per cent on this year's examination."

He walks away, leaving her to try to concentrate again on her work – tears staining the ink on the page in front of her, as the shock and shame of being caught gives way to the realisation that a zero score will inevitably leave her at the bottom of the class...

* I'd usually struggle with this concept – the idea of whacking a girl because she's not naturally bright seems unfair. But remember – this University only takes the very best students!

Confiscation

By Abel on 29 June 2009

It struck me that a list of the records of the Liverpool Girls' Reformatory that I discovered recently was missing one important category of documents:

    Letters, confiscated

Every letter written by the girls to their friends and families would, of course, have been checked by the staff. And any notes complaining about or discussing the conditions in the Reformatory – strict rules, birchings received – would have been confiscated.

Haron and I lay in bed on Sunday morning speculating on the contents of the file – after, that is, I'd given her six cuts of the cane (much deserved for her somewhat inebriated behaviour the evening before). Our conclusion was that the most interesting letter in the archive wouldn't be one intended for a recipient *outside* the Reformatory; rather, it'd be an intimate billet-doux from one girl to another:

    28 June 1922

    My dearest Eileen,

    It's so tough in here. Your kisses mean so much to me. I long for the secret moments we find together, for the gentle touch of your fingers.

    With love from your sweet friend,

    Flora

A good historian would doubtless correlate the date on the letter with the contents of the Admission Register to identify the girls – both aged 18, it would seem – and the Reformatory Punishment Book:

29 June 1922. Eileen Turner. Indecency. 12 strokes. Cane.

29 June 1922. Flora Denby. Indecency. 12 strokes. Cane.

Both entries would show the governor's signature. The only matter left for speculation would be where the punishments took place. In his office, bent over next to one another, taking alternate strokes? In his office, the first girl called in to be caned as the other listened, trembling, outside the door? Or my hunch: in the refectory, after lunch, bent over in full view of the other girls – the caning both punishment and deterrent?

Surprises

By Haron on 2 July 2009

I pondered surprises this morning: how much I don't like them where playing spanking scenes is concerned. I'm not sure if it's always been this way, but these days unless the scene is following very specific logic, I feel uncomfortable and thrown.

I'm not saying that I want to know exactly and in advance what's going to be happening to me: there should be enough room for manoeuvre for the top to use a slipper if he wants to, or a cane if he feels like it, or make me write lines, or whatever. But I really need to be told at the start how many issues we'll be dealing with, and what the rules are for the allocation of strokes.

For example, "and if you move, I'll give you an extra one", before a caning starts, is fine. "You've moved! It's an extra stroke!" is not fine, even if we've played before, and I'd had extra strokes for moving in previous scenes.

What particularly throws me is when I feel the punishment has come to its logical end, and I've suffered through it, then to hear "I'm not sure I've got through to you – I think another six are in order." I just shoot straight out of character, and feel like I've been lied to.

I wonder how it is for you? Do you like to be taken unawares?

Repaying his debt

By Abel on 11 July 2009

There are some scenes I'm not sure I'll ever get to play. But it doesn't stop me imagining them...

Picture the girl, being led along the corridor by her partner. They've travelled some distance. "I'd like to introduce you to a few friends,' he'd explained.

They stop in front of the final door. He knocks and waits. The door opens; he leads her in, clasping her wrist just a little too tightly. And before her eyes adjust to the darkness, it starts: hands cover her mouth, roughly; she's blindfolded.

He speaks, but not to her. "Repayment of my debt, gentlemen. I shall come back later, once you have finished with her."

An upper-class voice: firm, assertive: "You may leave us now." The door opens again, closes behind him.

She screams for help; the slap across her face buys her stunned silence. "Gentlemen," the voice murmurs softly: "Shall we?"

Hands. Everywhere, all at once – how many, she cannot tell. Touching, fondling, groping. She tries to fight her way out, but there are too many of them.

They strip her, tearing at buttons and cloth to bare her. And then the hands continue – probing, squeezing, penetrating.

The voice again: "Tie her down." And she feels herself being bent forward – over the back of a sofa, she guesses.

Ropes are applied to her wrists; she's pulled forward as they are secured. More ropes on her ankles; they too are tied tight, pulling her onto tiptoe, her legs parted, leaving her shamefully exposed.

She trembles, begs for mercy, even before the voice explains, "One stroke for every ten guineas owed." ('Guineas'? With what? How much did he owe? Did he know what they were going to do to her?)

And then the first cut, slicing, burning, agonising. The first of more-than-she-could count: the men swapping over every minute or so, as she pays his debt.

Then nothing. No strokes, no touching, no words. Just the agonising pain across her buttocks.

Eventually, he speaks again. "Shall we leave her, gentlemen?" And the sound of the door opening, and the group leaving.

The door shuts. She's alone. Sobbing.

And then the sound. A footstep behind her. A zip being opened, a belt buckle undone. And she realises she still has company, as he moves close behind her and she realises that the worst is still to come...

Waiting in the corner

By Haron on 12 July 2009

The other night we imagined a girl who misbehaved in class. The teacher, not normally known for his strictness, got tired of her fidgeting, leaning over to whisper and scrawling notes in the margins of her friends' books.

"Six with the slipper," he snapped finally.

Her mood dampened, she rose to walk to the front of the class, but the teacher lifted her palm to stop her.

"You don't think I should waste any more valuable classroom time on you, do you? Raise your skirt and face the wall. I will deal with you after the lesson."

And so she stood, alone in the corner, waiting for the bell to ring. She couldn't decide whether she would rather her knicker displaying shame was over sooner, or that it would last forever, putting off the descent of the slipper.

The bell would ring too soon. And yet, it wouldn't ring soon enough.

Queuing outside the headmaster's study
By Abel on 13 July 2009

Sometimes I think I have a cruel streak.

Take the little image that popped into my mind yesterday, while I was supposed to be writing a document for work. The door of the headmaster's study swings open; a girl emerges into the corridor, tearful and rubbing her bottom. A line of four, maybe five, of her friends waits outside.

"He wants you to go straight in," she tells the lass at the front of the queue, then whispers: "Good luck."

The door shuts. And within a moment, the freshly-punished girl is surrounded by her friends – comforting, consoling, wanting to know what it was like. She'd try not to worry them – "It wasn't too bad" masking the reality that being caned had been far, far worse than she'd anticipated.

And at that moment, a master would turn into the corridor. "What on earth is going on here?" The line would slink back against the wall, leaving the punished lass looking up at the Deputy Head. "You must know that talking outside the headmaster's office is strictly forbidden."

"Yes, sir. I mean, I've just been in trouble, and I've just come out, and my friends... Well, they were checking I was OK."

"I find it quite astonishing that a pupil can emerge from being punished by the headmaster, and flout a school rule within a matter of seconds."

"I'm sorry, sir."

"You can join the back of the queue, and once he's dealt with your colleagues, you can go in to see him again. Explain why I've sent you back. And I suspect the headmaster will teach you what a very dim view he'd take of a girl who misbehaves within minutes of being caned."

Refused boarding

By Abel on 17 July 2009

En route to Ireland last weekend to meet up with Emma Jane, I found myself sipping a coffee in the airport bar. By 6.55 a.m., the gentlemen at the next table were already on their second Guinness of the morning.

And what, I wondered, of girls on the school trip – a skiing expedition, a short trip to Paris to practise their French, an exchange visit with a sister school? Would they too sneak into the bar before their early flight? Might one of them drink just a little too much, and be refused boarding by vigilant airline staff?

The master in charge of the group would be called over; he'd provide the staff with the school address and money to fund a taxi, and would quickly call the headmaster before joining the rest of the group on the plane.

A caning would be inevitable – six slow, measured strokes on the bare that evening, once she'd sobered up. And then she'd head back to an empty dorm – her friends by now safely abroad – to sob herself to solitary sleep.

Dashing hero with a horse whip

By Haron on 18 July 2009

We were sitting in a restaurant about 20 minutes from our house, when the skies opened, and the rain poured down in sheets. When we'd left the house, it was bright sunshine, so we had no umbrella, and I was wearing sandals.

I love summer rain, but Abel made a miserable face. I tried to cheer him up: "It's an adventure!"

"It's not an adventure, we're going to be soaked to the skin. Unless… a girl goes out late, walking on the moors, a storm comes in, she has to be rescued. And punished."

"Yes," I said enthusiastically. "By a dashing man on a horse." I had a vision of a gentleman in breeches and a sodden white shirt sticking to his body, looking stormy as he helps the girl mount up in front of him.

"No," said Abel. "By her father."

That was an entirely different fantasy trying to encroach onto my Wuthering Heights.

"Dashing man!" I insisted. "On a horse!" White shirt sticking to a muscular torso, long black hair hanging in wet ropes…

"I'm allergic to horses," said Abel grumpily. "I can't suspend disbelief that far."

"Well, I can suspend disbelief far enough to cast you as a dashing man!" I blurted before stopping to think.

His face became very dangerous and, well… dashing. I squirmed, making an apologetic face.

And guess what – I got away with it. Probably because it was funny!

The point remains, though: rain to me is romance, Regency heroines and stormy heroes who spank and ravish them, making up the pain with an abundance of pleasure. Horses are optional, though.

In the headmaster's study

By Abel on 21 July 2009

Emma Jane's been keeping her readers posted with some wonderful accounts of the scenes she and I played during my recent visit to Ireland. But I'm going to dive in and blog about the very first scene of the weekend – which, indeed, was the first role-playing scene we'd played together.

–

"You wanted to see me, sir?"

The young lady in the door of the headmaster's office looked nervous – as well she might have been. (And oh, how delightfully authentic my playmate looked in her grey dress and blue school shirt. For a moment, I was that headmaster – not a mere role-player).

"Indeed." I didn't rise from my desk, but looked up from my paperwork, closing the folder in front of me (actually the hotel's brochure, masquerading as important papers for a forthcoming Governors' meeting). I came straight to the point: "Where were you this afternoon, Miss Woodhouse?"

She'd been at the dentist's, she told me. She'd had permission. (I'd known this, of course, the plot having been carefully agreed in advance).

"So why did one of my staff see you in the local shops?"

An excuse was quick to follow: "I popped into Top Shop, sir. But only for a moment." (Trying to disarm me. A confession hadn't been part of the plot. I thought quickly...). "Top Shop, eh? Then can you explain why you were seen in two other stores, at least half an hour apart?"

She couldn't. And now I played my joker: a call to the dentist had revealed that she hadn't ever had an appointment made for that afternoon.

I stood up, and walked across to the cupboard in which I'd stored the two school canes that were to be so well used over the weekend. I opened the door, took them out, and passed sentence: "I'm going to cane you, Miss Woodhouse. Six strokes for your truancy, and a further six for lying."

And so she bent over the arm of the sofa that the hotel had so conveniently provided, her knickers lowered, and I took up the lighter of the canes for the first half-dozen. Hard – on a cold bottom; clearly hurting. And then I paused, and picked up the second, heavier cane: "Those were for truancy. I view lying as a far more serious offence. And you have lied both with your excuse that you had a dental appointment, and then continued lying to me with your explanations this afternoon. I shall use the senior cane for the remaining six."

She protested (genuinely, I think!). But I was having none of it, and headmaster-me was determined to make these really count. She held her position bravely, although the strokes were delivered at full strength, and then it was all over.

"Stand up and adjust your clothing, and don't let me see you back here again." And so Emma Jane headed off – almost to the stairs leading out of the room, before turning with the biggest grin on her face and walking back over for a hug.

In the Master's study

By Haron on 28 July 2009

I went on a walking tour of Oxford colleges to indulge my fetish for old buildings. Abel chose retail therapy instead.

As I stood among a group in the Quad of New College,*
my phone buzzed with a text message:

> Girl on tour heads through the door marked 'strictly private'. Finds herself in Master's study as he returns. He decides to introduce her to the college's traditional means of dealing with disobedience.

This improved the already excellent tour a great deal. I could picture the chastened girl walking back through the cloisters, with the students lounging there giving her knowing looks...

*So called for being the oldest, obviously.

The sleepover
By Abel on 6 August 2009

I've been at my desk since before five this morning, working away diligently with just the occasional glance at kinky emails and blogs.

I've been rather distracted, though, by the sound of girls' voices drifting through the still morning air from a garden nearby.

Sooner or later, it struck me, there'll be different noises wafting on the breeze. For the friends at the summer holiday sleepover would have been allowed to spend the night in a tent, on condition that they behaved themselves and didn't disturb the neighbours.

When the father of the girl whose garden they're using is woken at this ungodly hour by their gossip and giggles, he'll take a very dim view of the situation. And when he reaches the garden and sees empty cider bottles littering the lawn around their tent...?

The lasses will be made to cut their own switches and bend over, before a chorus of strokes rings out – four each for the visitors, six for the young lady of the house. The subsequent short period of soft sobbing will be followed by blissful silence, and I'll be able to concentrate on my work again...

A costly ice cream

By Abel on 8 August 2009

I spent a wonderful summer's afternoon wandering around Stuttgart on Tuesday. The main square was bathed in sunlight; groups of friends played boules. I joined the locals sitting outside sipping a cold beer.

Later, I wandered through the city centre, noticing the groups of younger folk outside the ice cream bars. And an evil thought occurred to me.

For one of the lasses had been spared a switching for her atrocious report at the end of the school term by promising that she'd study flat out throughout the summer. But daddy had gone away on a business trip and wouldn't be back until late. With the coast clear, she'd be perfectly safe to slip into the town to spend the day with her friends.

Or so she thought.

For the business meeting had been cancelled at the last minute, and her father had found himself walking through the city centre with colleagues. He'd seen his daughter – who'd not noticed him.

By the time she bent over the end of the sofa that evening, after cutting a selection of switches from the back garden, it would not only be the poor report that had earned her a thrashing. There'd be the furtive trip out of the house to consider, too – never mind that she'd sworn blind to her father when he'd returned home that evening that she'd been studying diligently all day...

My tenth spanking anniversary
By Haron on 10 August 2009

My first spanking went like this.

At first, there were several months of anticipation. I was still living with my parents in Ukraine when I discovered the Internet world of spanking. I made friends, but they were all English-speakers, far away in the States and the UK. They may as well have been living on the moon, for how inaccessible the spanking scene looked to me, a 19-year-old student with no funds of my own.

A friend and regular correspondent Monty invited me to visit him in the summer holidays. I don't know how I convinced my father to let me go; he knew of my online friendships, but couldn't fathom what those older, respectable and foreign people could have found interesting about me. ("I love you, darling," he'd told me, "but teenagers are just not very interesting; it's a fact." I resented that at the time; ten years on I begin to see where he was coming from, though I'm not sure I'm old enough to agree with the sentiment.)

Be it as it may, I was allowed to go. Even then it wasn't just a matter of buying a plane ticket: I needed to apply for a British tourist visa, and wait, and go to an interview, and wait, and wait. Monty had to provide a sheaf of personal information to the visa people, but he didn't balk at writing on my behalf, and sending in papers that they really had no business looking at. It was a soul-melting bureaucratic hell, but I pushed through it, knowing that on the other side there was a magical prize waiting for me: finally, finally, I was going to get a spanking.

"You don't have to be spanked if you don't want to," Monty told me repeatedly, both online and in person, when finally I walked through the gate in Gatwick. Now I know how responsible and safe he was being, giving me control of the pace of my explorations. At the time, I thought he was insane. Not have a spanking? Not wanting to be spanked? After having craved it, reached for it, fought for it for months? I could barely wait, and might have thrown myself over his lap there in the airport.

We were both sensible, though, and waited until the excitement of the first day of my visit had dampened a little. The following morning he turned into my Uncle Monty, a familiar figure from our chatroom role-play. He sat on the chair, and pulled me over his lap, and it felt so real and natural as though I'd been doing this my whole life.

Monty's lap was the most comfortable place in the world, even when his hand slapped down onto my bottom, stinging quite a bit. I was so happy, I didn't even dare cry out or kick, because I didn't want to spoil the perfection of the moment. He let me up eventually, and gave me a hug. I couldn't keep to the role of a naughty niece: I was grinning like mad, the happiest girl in the world.

There were more spankings that week, of course. I was introduced to implements, and wore a makeshift school uniform, though it hadn't occurred to me beforehand that people might dress up when they role-played. I was given some spectacular first-timer bruises, even through my knickers, which I was still too shy to take down at any point. I misbehaved a little. I reported about my joy at the message board where Monty and I had met, and felt warmth and support from the more experienced players, all of whom had been there before.

This was all later. My first spanking – that perfect moment of joy – happened exactly ten years ago, today.

'The English Experience'

By Abel on 12 August 2009

Standing just beyond the security checks as I headed home through Stuttgart airport last week was a very cute young lady, in a neat uniform of short grey skirt and pale blue polo top. She held a sign aloft for all to see – 'The English Experience'. Every few minutes, lost-looking teenage girls wandered up to her, and were pointed towards the ever-growing group where they made their introductions.

Little, I thought, did they realise the nature of the 'experience' that lay ahead of them when they reached our green, pleasant and ever-so-wet lands. For this was to be a little more than the simple language course that they'd envisaged. Their parents had paid out the extortionate fees knowing that their time in England was to be as much about discipline as it would be about language.

The girls would be staying in dorms at a fine public school, deep in some rural valley. There'd be a group meeting that first evening, at which they were introduced to the school's more senior masters, who had given up their summer holidays to supervise the 'experience'. The rules for the month ahead would be explained; the strictness of the regime would leave many shocked.

And then the girls who'd been observed sneaking away at the airport to head for the bar or the glass-fronted 'smoking zone' would find themselves called to the front, where they'd be lectured, and publicly caned in front of the group.

The following morning, they'd each be called in turn into housemasterial studies. A folder would be taken out containing reports from their school and parents; a lengthy discussion about their conduct would follow. There'd be tears, and apologies, and vows to do better –

even before they'd been told to bend over and touch their toes...

The right kind of school skirt

By Haron on 19 August 2009

In my dream I was a girl preparing to go to boarding school for the first time. Mother took me to a specialist uniform shop, where all the essentials, from socks to hair ribbons, could be bought, plus a trunk to store all of this.

A kindly shop assistant helped me choose a skirt of the correct length. My mother said: "I thought, the rule is that the skirt should reach the floor when she kneels."

"Never mind that," said the shop assistant. "The main thing is for the skirt to cover enough when she is touching her toes for the cane. The first-formers are allowed to keep their skirts down; well, just make sure it reaches far enough down. Would you like to try, dear?"

And so I tried on endless skirts, bending over with my back to the mirror, considering the view I would present from the back. In my chest, there ran a secret, naughty thrill: I was a big girl, going to a big school where they used the cane.

Burning down the house

By Abel on 20 August 2009

"Hi. Might you be able to send an iron and ironing board up to my room?"

It didn't seem an unreasonable request for me to make at the posh resort in which we've been staying on holiday out in Cyprus. But clearly I was expecting far too much:

"No, sir. We don't let people have irons in the rooms. Policy: health and safety."

The lady on the other end of the line directed me to an ironing room, four floors up at the far end of the hotel. I explained that I could, honestly, be trusted with an iron – having avoided burning down any of the chain's hotels in the hundreds of nights I'd spent with them in recent years. She reluctantly agreed to speak to her manager.

A few moments, she called me back:

"Hi. It's Daniella from reception. I can send up an iron and ironing board after all." She sounded a little embarrassed as she continued: "But my manager's told me to phone you to tell you that you have to be responsible with it."

Me? Responsible? "It's OK," I reassured her, as she giggled. "I won't brand my wife with it. That's not my thing."

–

The following morning, I woke particularly early and decided to head down to the pool. I had the place to myself for half an hour – and I always enjoy a good paddle. As I swam, I reflected on the events that had no doubt transpired there just a few hours before.

Very late the previous night: a group of lasses from the hotel staff had found themselves walking past the pool – in which they were forbidden to swim – their duties finished for the day, the guests all safely despatched back to their rooms.

What could be more natural than a quick skinny-dip? They stripped, swam, giggled. Only they'd bargained without the CCTV cameras. The security guard and duty manager soon appeared at the side of the pool, and ordered them out. As the girls stood there – dripping, naked, covering themselves – the manager informed them that such blatant misconduct would be bound to lead to their dismissal when they were brought before the General Manager the following morning.

When they protested, pleaded, he relented and sent the security man to fetch the cane from his office. And the staff were lined up, touching their toes, on the edge of the pool, each given ten stripes and sent on their way in disgrace.

The temple whippings

By Abel on 22 August 2009

One of the nicer features of our Cypriot resort was the cave area at the end of one of the pools. (Yes, 'ca*ve*', for those perverts amongst you who just instinctively read that as the 'ca*ne* area'). Swimming through the stone arches, one found oneself in a sheltered area, with waterfalls, ledges on which to sit, and a large mosaic of some Greek god. This, needless to say, sparked my imagination, for surely this design must have been inspired by some ancient Greek site?

Let's suppose that some misfortune had befallen the locals – a poor harvest; a drought; an outbreak of sickness, perhaps. Clearly, this would have to have been caused by the gods expressing their displeasure.

The remedy would be clearly set out in the learned books. A maiden from the town would be selected by lot and sent to swim out (naked, of course) across the lake to the temple. There, the high priest would be waiting for her, taking her into the cave. He'd tie her before the high altar, and would whip her until he thought that the gods would be pleased by the demonstration of their subjects' submission. And then the girl would be untied, and made to swim back across the lake. The waiting crowd would compliment her on her bravery; she'd be given wine and food and massaged with soothing oils.

And what if the gods had not been placated? Well, naturally, the next maiden would be sent across the pool the following day, whipped harder and sent home – and so on until the gods chose to spare the village from whatever disaster was befalling them.

The morning after the celebration
By Haron on 25 August 2009

One evening last week we drove through our normally quiet town, and found that dozens of nicely dressed teenagers were out in the streets, partying. It wasn't the weekend. It wasn't a public holiday. We were puzzled for a minute, until we realised that this was the day that school-leavers all over the country had received their exam results.

This explained the partying, of course – but not excused it, in the case of a particular girl, who had been told in no uncertain terms that she must not go out without her father's permission. Ever.

"But everybody was going to the club, Daddy," she would plead the next morning, bleary-eyed from staying up dancing all night. "Don't you think I had something to celebrate, with my three As?"

"Undoubtedly," her father would say dryly. "But the manner of your celebration was unacceptable. You know I wouldn't have allowed you to stay out until dawn – is that why you didn't ask for permission to go out?"

She would sigh, resigned. Of course, this was it: she had known that had she asked, Father would have told her to come home at one o'clock at the latest. That was why she'd risked it, hoping that in the morning he would let it slip just this once.

But of course, he wouldn't. All too soon his little girl would be going away to university, and he would be particularly keen to instil some good habits in her, such as going to bed in the evening and getting up in the morning, not vice versa.

"Have a shower, put on your pyjamas and wait for me in your bedroom," he would say. "I will come to deal with you shortly. And by the way... you're grounded for the weekend."

She would trudge to the bathroom and stand under the shower, hot water mixing with tears. It would be the hairbrush, of course. Bedtime spankings were always given with a hairbrush, never mind that she was going to bed at 7 in the morning.

In an awesome crash after yesterday's celebrations, she wouldn't feel very grown up at all.

Cumulative effect

By Haron on 29 August 2009

Yesterday we ventured to join the local library in our new town. The nice librarian person explained about borrowing, the facilities and such things, and finally showed us a table of fines for returning books late.

"It's £0.70 per book per day. It may not seem like much, but it does build up, so..." She gave us a meaningful glare.

I imagined her give a completely different warning.

"It's just one stroke of the cane, per book per day. It doesn't seem like much, but when you have to report to the council offices for your strokes, even one will seem like too much."

...What? I'm sure librarians would love to introduce corporal punishment for late returns.

The caning machine
By Abel on 31 August 2009

The latest addition to my movie library features two cute models being thrashed in turn by a spanking machine. They're tied to the whipping frame; the device is positioned behind them, to the side. At the touch of a computerised button, the machine whips the cane forwards, horizontally, across its target, then back into place ready for the next stroke. The machine adjusts the height of the strokes, little by little, leaving perfect parallel stripes across the girls' behinds.

Haron hates the lack of a human touch, whereas I found the very dehumanising of the process to be quite fascinating. So much, so, in fact, that I've been picturing wider applications for the machines.

See, flogging one girl at a time seems an awfully inefficient use of prison officers' time. I'd propose a large room, equipped to punish ten or more offenders in a session. The young women, wearing prison uniforms, would be escorted in by the officers, and made to line up. Their names would be read out in turn – once a girl was called, she'd be expected to step forward and strip, before being sent to stand behind her designated punishment station.

Once all of the girls were in place, the officers would tour the room, strapping them tightly into position. The machines would be positioned carefully, and checked. For the girls, the lengthy wait – as their fellow inmates were readied for punishment – would be filled with trepidation.

The officers would then retire to the control panel at the back of the room, and would enter details of each girl's name and offence. The computer would check whether an offender had been flogged before. And then it would calculate the number of strokes due in each case. Once all of the sentences had been worked out, the senior officer would type in the instruction to commence the punishments, and the machines would spring into life.

Two or three girls might feel the cut of the cane at precisely the same moment, but the strokes would be unpredictable in pattern. Caned immediately before one's nearest neighbour, then moments after, then before, then at the same time. Twenty seconds apart, then forty, then ten, then three in immediate succession. Severity varying, from very hard to the machine's hardest.

The near-silent workings of the mechanisms – amidst the sounds of sobbing – would mean that a girl would have no way of knowing whether a particular swish would be coming her way, until the very moment of impact. And whilst she'd have a vague idea of the likely number of strokes (ten to twenty being par for the course), a girl would have no idea of the total tally calculated by the computer – and hence, after the first ten, of whether any given stroke had been her last.

(Oh. I think I've just scared Haron).

The dorm inspection

By Abel on 4 September 2009

It was a dark, wet, windy morning... Walking through deserted streets to the local train station at 5.30am yesterday really was a miserable experience. Not a light in a single window; it really did seem as though I was the only person awake at such an ungodly hour.

To cheer myself up, my crook-handled umbrella caned countless imaginary girls as I strolled. (Hey, there was no-one around, OK?). And then inspiration struck. For surely this would be precisely the time at which the prefects in the local girls' boarding school would conduct a surprise early-morning dorm inspection?

They'd burst in, unannounced, and flick on the bright lights. The girls in the room would be made to climb groggily from their beds; they'd stand watching (and trembling) as the inspection took place.

Some would be sent back to sleep, everything being in order. Others would be found guilty of minor offences – clothes strewn on the floor rather than folded neatly on their bedside chair; wearing non-regulation pyjamas. They'd be made to bend over the end of their bed for a sound whacking with the prefectorial plimsoll.

And the remaining few? Those foolish girls whose bedside tables contained stashes of illicit contraband – cigarettes, alcohol? They'd be made to put on their dressing gowns and go and wait in silence until their housemaster arrived in his study that morning, knowing that a caning was inevitable.

A governess or a tutor?

By Haron on 8 September 2009

There are days when a girl just needs some help with her work. I'm incredibly busy just now, and as I split various assignments into pieces of "homework", I imagine having a strict person who would sit next to me as I work, pointing out mistakes, praising good work, and giving me an occasional smack when my gaze starts drifting towards the window.

The only thing is, I can't decide whether this person should be my governess, who spends all day with me, making sure that everything I do is just right – or a tutor, who arrives at an appointed hour specifically to help with my homework.

Both are strict. Both have my best interest in mind, even as they smack my bottom for some little misdeed or another. Except, if I have a tutor, he could also appeal to my governess afterwards if my efforts are not up to scratch, and then I'd have both of them to explain myself to.

I can't really choose. But I'm clearly in need of one or the other...

The strict choirmaster

By Haron on 11 September 2009

With Abel being away for a few days, I can watch girly TV, and so I indulged myself with "The Choir" on BBC1. In this programme, a handsome young man tries to build a community choir in a run-down south-eastern town.

Now, I loved singing in a choir when I was at school, but we never had a good-looking guy as our choirmaster – instead, we had a variety of boring women. I would have enjoyed the singing even more if the man in charge was handsome in an authoritative way, and quietly stern.

I would, I think, particularly dread being late to practice. He would ignore me until a convenient time to break, and then give me a disappointed look and then nod for me to join my section. From this silent acknowledgement I would know that my lateness was noted, and that after practice I was to come and see him, alone.

I would wait in my place as the rest of the choir filed out. The pianist would gather her music and leave too, a little smile on her lips as she passed me. Only then would the choirmaster speak to me for the first time.

"We've been here before," he would say, reaching into the inside pocket of his jacket for a tawse. "I'm very disappointed in you. Come here."

I would know exactly what to do. I would bend down and put my elbows on the piano stool, feel him lift my woollen skirt out of the way. The tawse would tap my bottom gently at first, and he would say, "Yes?"

I would cringe and sing out, to a tune of practice arpeggio: "I-must-not-be-late!" A crack against my bottom would make me hiss and bite onto my lip.

"Again!"

"I-must-not-be-late!" I would sing, moving up a tone. Another crack; this time I wouldn't be able to contain a whimper.

"Again!"

So I would move up a scale: seven notes, seven strokes of the tawse, with the eighth and final one aimed straight over the top of my thighs. At this point my eyes would be slightly moist; I would try to cover this up as I painfully unbent, and would fail.

"Good girl," the choirmaster would say, offering me a hug. "Don't do this again. Yes?"

"Yes, sir." Uncomfortably, I would bury my face in his jacket for a moment of comfort.

After which I would go home, and fantasise about receiving other comforts at his hands.

Imagining the reformatory

By Abel on 16 September 2009

Sunday morning, lazing in bed. Our talk turned to reformatories.

On their admission, I suggested, the girls would be lined up facing the wall, hands on heads, and ordered to remain silent. One of their number would be selected by an officer and taken into the adjoining room; the door would be shut firmly behind.

The remaining girls would hear mutters of conversation; a shower running, perhaps; the sounds and yelps of a strapping; more words being exchanged. And then the door would open and the first inmate would retake her place in the line – only by now, naked, shivering and sore. And then the next girl would be selected...

We moved on to darker places: a line of girls, tied down, each having been soundly flogged. The senior officer would call his colleagues to attention, and invite them to select the girl of his choice. Each guard would take his reward for his exertions with the whip, the girls bound in such a position as to be unable to see who was behind them. And therefore, presumably, being unable to look any of the officers in the eye for the remainder of her sentence...

Bavarian spankings

By Abel on 20 September 2009

To Munich, briefly, last week to speak at a conference. Sadly, I was accompanied by one of my team, so the trip was kink-free – although my imagination, of course, continued to work along its usual lines.

As one does, we headed to one of the city's famous old beer cellars for the evening – where my resolution to spend an entire month without drinking alcohol came to an abrupt end. (Hey, four weeks is a month, OK?)

Our fellow drinkers and diners were an eclectic bunch – lots of lederhosen, girls in traditional Bavarian dresses (oh, how they needed pulling over a lap to be spanked), and a group of twenty or so youngsters that appeared at the next table towards the end of the evening.

I'm not sure what the legal drinking age is in Germany, but I'm guessing it's 18 – and none of our neighbours could have been more than 16. Since they were sitting just inside the door, any passing policeman glancing inside would certainly have spied them. I pictured the scene – the Polizei appear, the group scatters, some escaping into the street but a handful of the young ladies being caught by the cops and the waiters.

They'd beg not to be arrested and, this being a traditional place, a compromise would be agreed. They'd be led to an upstairs room; they'd be ordered to bend over next to one another over the side of a long oak table, and to take down their trousers and knickers. An old, heavy, well-worn strap would be fetched from the manager's office, and six merciless strokes each would prove most effective before the punished, tearful troupe were marched back through the restaurant and out onto the street.

Experimental caning

By Haron on 21 September 2009

We were about to go out for Sunday lunch, when something compelled me to say: "Wouldn't it be a shame if it hurt me to sit down in the pub?" Abel immediately agreed that it would be a dreadful shame, and ordered me to his office.

I didn't start to regret my impulsiveness until I saw him pick out a really thick cane, and heard that he had an experiment in mind.

"I've been proofreading my story," he said, "and in it a girl struggles to take six hard strokes of the cane without leaping up. I want to see how this works in practice."

Oh, great, I thought as I pushed down my jeans and knickers. An endurance test, just what I wanted... why did I volunteer for this, again?

"If you move out of position, I will repeat the stroke," said Abel. I silently promised myself that I would not move out of position for anything.

The experiment went like this: he swung the cane and cracked it down with awesome force and noise. I saw stars and screamed a lot. He swung and cracked again, I screamed some more. At one point Abel asked me if I could keep the noise down, at which I asked him if he could keep the pain down. I guess, it was a "no" on both counts.

The results of the experiment revealed that I can, indeed, stay down for an extremely hard half-dozen strokes. But I'm going to scream my head off. It's either moving or jumping about – the reaction has to go somewhere. So now he knows.

Sitting down in the pub, as well as in the car there and back, was absolutely delicious.

The Punishment Centre

By Abel on 22 September 2009

Now *that* was a hot scene. Young Grace (our friend Scarlett, in fact) had been sent her formal notice from the Punishment Centre, requiring her to report at a given time. For the offence of graffiti: 15 strokes of the cane.

Miss Cadogan (Haron) drove off to the station shortly before the time of the appointment, to meet the girl (already in role). And Punishment Officer Jenkins sat back and waited in my office, for the first part of the proceedings were entirely in Miss Cadogan's capable hands (although carefully planned by us both in advance).

I heard the front door open and close; footsteps on the stairs; heard the door of the back bedroom shut firmly. There, I knew, Grace would be made to strip; she'd then be taken to the punishment room (aka our bedroom) and tied in position ready to be punished.

A few minutes later came a knock: Miss Cadogan to see me. "Your 9pm appointment is ready, sir," she informed me. We went into the room together; Grace was tied in position, naked, her ankles apart and bound to the foot of the bed, her hands drawn forward by a tight rope to the bed's head. I couldn't see her face; she couldn't see me.

Miss Cadogan handed me the clipboard; I scanned the form carefully, noted that Grace had signed to confirm that she understood the punishment that was to come. And then my assistant left the room, for the whipping to begin.

I lectured, of course: how vandalism couldn't be tolerated; how I intended to teach her a lesson. I noted how she had existing faint cane marks (my doing at our previous play session), and that she must therefore be a bad girl in need of firm correction.

I picked up the heavy, whippy, dragon cane (one of the more severe in my collection), and administered the first cut. Hard. It striped her beautifully. And then continued – pausing between administering her stripes, lecturing, varying the height at which the strokes fell but never varying their intensity. She counted each, thanking me, her trembling tone (and her "owwww"s) reaffirming the efficacy of the punishment.

And then it was over, and Miss Cadogan was called back in to help untie her and conclude the proceedings – the photographs, for the official records; a (much shakier) signature from Grace to acknowledge that she had been punished; one from me to confirm that I'd dealt with her. Only, the young lady disobeyed an order to keep her hands on her head, thus earning herself one additional stroke: back over the bed, the whack as hard as its predecessors.

And then it was time to hug, and rest, before Scarlett foolishly confessed that she'd never been spanked with a hairbrush and the rest of the evening played out...

Reaching for the hairbrush

By Haron on 25 September 2009

Abel was spanking me over his knee on the bed, and I was making lots of squeaking noises, as I do.

"I don't know what you're complaining about," said he. "This isn't a hard spanking. I'll show you what a hard spanking is like; get me that hairbrush." And he pointed at his Mason Pearson lying on top of the chest of drawers a good metre away from the bed. "Or," he added considerately, "you can hand me that one if you want," and he pointed at my light paddle brush, easily within reach on the bedside table.

"It's OK, I'll go get the Mason Pearson," I said, clambering out of my comfy spanking position and out of bed. "The other one is full of hair, eww."

Don't think I'm a slob and don't clean my brush. It's just that my hair is really long; if there're even three stray hairs remaining after cleaning, the brush looks like it's been used by the wild woman of Borneo. It's just not good for spanking.

Maybe one of the features of a good spanko girl should be that she always keeps her brush pristine, just in case it was needed.

It would be a lovely ritual, actually: cleaning the hairbrush every morning. Time-consuming, but lovely.

Owning up

By Abel on 26 September 2009

The headmaster, in my day dreams at the back of my conference in Germany last week, was standing at the front of the classroom of twenty or so girls, wearing his gown and flexing a crook-handled cane. "This is your final chance," he warned. "If the culprit doesn't own up now, I shall cane you all."

The girls looked at each other, and slowly one of their number rose to her feet. "It was me, sir," she confessed. "Then you'll accompany me to my study," came the icy reply.

Later in the day, one of the masters would overhear a conversation in the playground that he reported to the Head. The girl who'd been caned hadn't, it seemed, been the actual offender – rather, she'd admitted guilt to save the whole class from punishment. And the two real miscreants, who'd now confessed to their friends, had escaped scot-free save for the unbearable guilt.

The three girls concerned were quickly called before the headmaster. The lass he'd punished in the morning was shown in first, to learn the painful way that he took an even dimmer view of lying than he did of the offence for which he'd caned her that morning. And she'd discover that six strokes on the bare would hurt far more than their predecessors over her skirt.

The two real culprits would then be called in in turn. Blazers removed, skirts lifted, knickers lowered, they'd each receive twelve of the very best with his thickest cane, before being sent back to their classroom in utter shame.

Summarily caned

By Haron on 29 September 2009

I got out of bed at my normal weekday hour of 7am, except it was Sunday, so I didn't have to actually be properly up. I padded to the bathroom, waving good morning to Abel (who gets up at the crack of dawn no matter what day it is), and then, coming back, I told him that I wasn't, in fact, up: I was still in bed.

"Why are you not in the dormitory in the middle of the night?" he demanded, getting up from his chair. "Wandering around the corridors like that is not acceptable. Come with me."

He escorted me to the bedroom, where he picked up a conveniently available cane. "Over the bed," he said.

I leaned over the edge of the bed, bit on my lip, not wishing to wake the neighbourhood, and winced through a swift, stingy caning. "Ow, sir," I said meekly when it was over.

"Don't let it happen again," he said. "Get back into bed, young lady."

And so I did. The rest of that morning's dreams were very pleasant.

American education

By Abel on 30 September 2009

A work acquaintance told tale t'other day of a colleague who's just relocated from London to the States, together with wife and teenage daughter.

It would be a few weeks into her first term at her new school that the call would come from the principal's office, asking him to pick up his daughter immediately for some grave offence. "I'd usually paddle students for this, but since you signed the form refusing permission for me to use corporal punishment, I have no choice but to suspend her," he'd explain.

"What form?"

"It was one of the sheaf of papers you returned to us before your daughter started."

And so the saga would unfold: the daughter who'd offered to read all the paperwork and so helpfully to fill it in, so all her father had to do was sign. Her failure in so doing to mention the disciplinary form, knowing that her father would doubtless condone a sound paddling were she to misbehave.

The journey to the school to pick up both the girl and a fresh punishment form. A stern lecture that evening, before his belt was taken off and folded double. Tears and cuddles afterwards. And a trip to the principal's office the following morning to deliver her fresh form, then bend over his desk to be paddled hard across her jeans.

Caned by the leading man
By Haron on 1 October 2009

The most awesome dream ever: I was playing a parlour maid in the theatre, and the leading man was Alan Rickman. There was a scene where he caned me, which not only did I get to enjoy as we rehearsed and researched it, but also got to repeat night after night in front of the theatre's audience.

I wish I could go back to that dream and have it every night!

Saturday school, Japanese-style
By Abel on 4 October 2009

Saturday, our first full day in Japan – and our hotel's club lounge thankfully has wi-fi. We decided to take an easy introduction to Tokyo, so wandered into Ginza, one of the main shopping areas, where Haron's stationery fetish was duly indulged.

We spied a fair few delightfully-uniformed schoolgirls as we wandered. My darling wife expressed sympathy with their plight: "It's mean that they have to go to school on a Saturday." Needless to say, I jumped to the more obvious conclusion – that these were the girls sentenced to a Saturday detention.

They'd start the day in a queue outside a classroom; the duty master would take in the first girl, bend her over the teacher's table at the front of the room, cane her soundly, and then send her to sit at one of the wooden desks to start writing an essay of atonement for whatever transgression had led to her punishment. The next offenders would be called in one by one, and each dealt with in a similar manner.

As lunchtime drew near, the girls would be made to come to the front of the class in turn to read their apologies aloud. Should the master be less than satisfied with the length, content or tone of their work, a further, harder caning would follow, this time on the bare.

The imperial collection

By Abel on 8 October 2009

By a stroke of fortuitous timing, our visit to the Tokyo National Museum coincided with the opening of a major new exhibition showing – for the first time in public – the best artworks from the Japanese imperial collection.

It was crowded, as you would expect, not least with parties of schoolgirls obediently studying the exhibits. Except, we surmised, for two of their number who would have sneaked outside and hidden away for a smoke – relying on their friends to let them copy the answers to the quiz they were supposed to have filled out whilst touring the exhibition halls.

Only, unusually, their teacher would ask for the completed forms when the girls came to board the bus, rather than at the end of the journey. The two young ladies would present blank sheets; the schoolmaster would scent the aroma of tobacco; a search of their blazer pockets would reveal the half-smoked packet of cigarettes.

They'd be sent back inside to do the work, naturally – whilst their classmates sat (increasingly bored, in forced silence) on the coach, awaiting their return. And, needless to say, when they did eventually get back, by now very late, to the high school grounds, they'd be marched in front of the headmaster to explain what had transpired, and hence to be caned.

A caning lesson

By Haron on 11 October 2009

An item on the news about the lack of male teachers in schools these days, and how it's a bad thing. I imagine a predominantly female common room watching the news during the lunch break, commenting to each other that an extra man or two would certainly be nice.

"We could delegate some of the canings," a young teacher straight out of college would say wistfully. "In my old school the housemaster did all the caning, and he was fearsome." She'd blush as she realises what she has just admitted to.

"My dear," a slightly older teacher would say with a smile. "You don't need a man to deliver a fearsome caning. You just need skill and confidence, and that comes with practice and a little bit of inspiration. Come see me at four. I will show you something."

The young teacher would walk to her older friend's classroom after the final bell, making her way through a throng of departing girls, feeling not unlike she used to when she walked to her housemaster's study after the end of lessons. She would stop just before knocking on the door, and remember that she can just enter unasked.

"Here you are," her older friend would say. "Take a seat. My miscreant won't be long if she knows what's good for her."

Sure enough, a fifth-form girl would appear soon, her presence announced by a timid knock. She would look too nervous, too preoccupied to ask about the presence of another teacher in the room.

A short discussion of her misdeed would follow: passing notes in class, after having been warned about it before. She would apologise with tears in her voice, clearly knowing what's coming.

"I'm glad to hear you are sorry," her teacher would say. "But this time, I'm afraid, I need to impress upon you the need to focus in class, and not to distract other girls with your silliness. Raise your skirt, please, and bend over my desk."

The young teacher would watch the girl reluctantly bend forward with her knickers tightly stretched over her bottom. The older teacher would pick up the cane that every classroom has hanging on a nail by the board and walk back and forth behind the girl, only the clicking of her heels breaking the silence. Finally she would take her position and tap the cane lightly on the girl's behind, taking aim, before bringing the instrument up in a graceful arc and whipping it down with a crack.

The younger teacher would take mental notes throughout this intense display. She would mark her friend's complete composure, her unhurried manner, the wait between the strokes, the comforting hand on the small of the girl's back when the sobbing became desperate. She would try to remember the short lecture that came after the girl, dishevelled and undone, was allowed to rise, followed by a kindly offer of a hug, gratefully accepted. An edifying spectacle indeed, she would think, comparing it to her own stumbling attempts to cane some of her unruly pupils.

After the teachers are alone again, the older one would smile to the younger friend. "There you are," she would say. "It's all that, and a bit of practice on the cushions. No need to hand it over to men, see?"

"Thank you," the young woman would say. "I see now."

And she would. For even though she was only a spectator, she would have to admit that her pulse was beating just as fast as it used to after the encounter with her housemaster. She would go home, and think about authority, and practise on cushions.

An abundance of birthday spankings
By Haron on 12 October 2009

So, today's my birthday, and I've already got a very sore bottom as a result. That's how it works. Birthday = presents, of course, but also, birthday = spanking, and plenty of it.

But today's soreness doesn't begin to compare to the state my bottom was in the weekend before we left for Japan, when I returned home after sleeping over at some friends' house – and discovered that Abel had gathered up a huge crowd of our friends for a surprise birthday party for me.

Normally I don't play much at parties, as I'm too shy to ask, but this was actually all about me, so there was no need to be modest. I bravely decided to ask every top in attendance for a birthday spanking.

My goodness, what a fool I was to think that a birthday spanking necessarily consists of the number of strokes corresponding to one's age, plus one for luck. Granted, a couple of people stuck to the 30 + 1 formula, but some very nicely warmed me up with 5 different implements before the count even started, and some decided to dispense with the counting altogether, walloping me for what it was worth. Seven "birthday spanking" sessions later, plus two spankings for general naughtiness, I was so sore that pulling my knickers up was almost unbearably painful. Plus, it was getting late. My ambitious plan had proved to be quite unrealistic in the end.

I used to think that birthday spankings were boring, as there was no psychological reason behind them. Unless I was spanked for something in particular, there was, to me, no point in doing it. I get it now, though: the reason for a birthday spanking is that you're with friends who care for you, and want you to have a good time. Even when "a good time" means being so sore that you wake yourself up turning over in your sleep.

Birthday spankings are good. Yes.

* It was a school-themed event in everything including the massive birthday cake, which was decorated with a book of school rules, a teacher's mortarboard and a pencil that may have been a cane. I was in heaven.

Samurai discipline

By Haron on 27 October 2009

Lest anybody think we have been completely idle on our Japanese holiday, let me assure you that we have not lacked for educational experiences. One such – and by far the best – was a lesson on samurai swordsmanship.

The stuff we learned was an introduction to stage-fighting as opposed to the sort of fighting where you try to actually chop up the opponent. Before unleashing a blow, you are supposed to utter a warning cry each time, so that your sparring partner knows to get out of the way. You bounce the blows instead of following them through for impact. That sort of thing.

Our instructor had choreographed the fights on Kill Bill Vol 1, and runs a sword-fighter acting troupe. He has a slight stature and a gentle manner, yet you wouldn't even dream of doing anything to displease him. You instantly know that you're in the presence of a master of his craft. Oh, how my submissive little heart was longing for a proper lesson, instead of the tourist-friendly version with its inherent not entirely deserved praise!

There was an assistant instructor, a young man who had an impressive way with his sword, and a deliciously subservient manner towards the master. I mentally cast him as my brother apprentice in a demanding training programme: somebody who would go out of his way to protect me from the master's wrath, and yet gently nudge me forward with my learning.

The wooden swords being inspiring fantasy fodder, I also imagined myself learning to use the cane from a renowned disciplinarian. "This is the stroke you use. Flick the wrist, you're not chopping wood. Good. Now aim for this stripe on the cushion; a hundred repetitions, please... Good. Now the back-hand."

The strictness of the samurai swordsman
By Abel on 28 October 2009

Like Haron, I loved our afternoon with the samurai swordsmen.

The master had an impressive presence. Short, calm, softly spoken – and unbelievably authoritative as he walked amidst the group, adjusting their posture, correcting the position in which they held their blades until they were just so. I'm looking forward to applying some of his techniques the next time I have a cane in my hand, as I'm sure they'll cross over from one art to another...

One exercise had us repeating the practice movement that a samurai would have undertaken 2,000 times each morning – lifting the sword high, practicing a blow: "forward, cut, back, lift…" We only performed the routine 100 times, as did the girl in my post-workshop fantasies after I woke the following morning. See, the cutest of the young ladies in the class had shown quite an aptitude, and had returned to train alone with the master before dawn each morning. He had been unhappy with her attitude from the start of the session; she'd already earned one crisp slap across the face.

His discontent was evident as she performed the 100-cut warm-up, her routine ragged, her swordsmanship untidy. At the end, he left her standing, the heavy sword held high, uncomfortably above her head. A long, meaningful silence.

Eventually, she broke it: "Are you displeased with me, master?"

"Did I give you permission to speak?"

"No, master."

Silence once more, broken eventually by his instruction to her to take her sword to the corner of the room, and bring back the cane in its place.

"I will not accept such ill-disciplined work."

"No, master."

"Nor can I comprehend how you could show such disrespect as to only perform 96 cuts, rather than the required 100."

"I'm sorry, master."

He'd untie her belt and open her kimono, pushing it back over her shoulders; it fell to the floor at her feet, leaving her naked in front of him. He'd order her to pick it up, to fold it neatly, then to bend over and grasp her ankles. "You will count – accurately, this time – to 100, whilst learning that I demand rather more application from my pupils than you have offered me this morning."

"Yes, master."

And so he'd punish her, quickly and rhythmically: no individual stroke too hard, but their cumulative effect quite agonising as she counted towards her tally.

Afterwards, he'd make the student stand. "Go and get dressed, and leave. There is nothing more I can teach you this morning." And she would be dismissed, bowing low before him and thanking him for her lesson.

The crackdown and its consequences
By Abel on 30 October 2009

Back home from our marathon trip, and it seems that we've been missing interesting announcements back home whilst we've been in Japan. According to the BBC:

> Thousands of teenagers had a total of 5,171 litres of alcohol confiscated in a summer crackdown on binge drinking, the government has said.
>
> As part of a £1.4m campaign, more than 3,500 youngsters in 69 "priority areas" of England were stopped between July and September.

What I love about this, from an Abel-can-pervert-anything-to-create-scene-potential perspective is the subsequent comment, though: apparently "more than 1,800 parents were informed".

Not only, it seems was young Haron not studying in the library on the evening in question – but she was with that boy she promised she wouldn't ever see again. And – shock, horror – she's not teetotal after all. Indeed (gasps of horrified astonishment) she must have been buying booze underage. Get upstairs immediately, young lady...

Caned at the Approved School

By Abel on 7 November 2009

Thursday, 8.46pm

About to play ... I've just been up to my study, and prepared the headmaster's office. We're in the Oxfordshire Approved School; Miss Temple (Haron) has just caught young Miss Grey (Graham) trying to escape – indeed, more seriously, having tried to organise a mass escape of the girls resident here. When the door knocks, in a few minutes, they'll be standing outside in role.

The curtain's drawn; the desk is set ready; canes are in the stand. (I wonder which I'll use? One of the more severe ones, I think). Ropes are carefully placed – just out of sight, in case I decide that a girl needs her ankles tying to hold her in place.

I've changed, wearing a suit. I've even put on a tie for the occasion. (Amusingly, I only ever seem to wear ties these days when spanking girls – never for business!). Our cat's just wandered in to see what's going on – I think I'd better throw her out...

Oh, how I love the anticipation that comes from being on the verge of playing a good scene.

9.08pm

Scene over. Girl soundly caned; to be comforted. Notes on the scene to be compared. That was good!!

Friday morning, 6.26am

As is so often the case, I'm the first person to wake in the house. The memories of an excellent scene flooded back as soon as I walked into my office. The cane's hanging on the back of the chair; my computer screen still reads "Oxfordshire Approved School".

Miss Grey was surprisingly defiant, given her predicament. I had to explain that the Approved School regime was designed to help her – that her delinquency before joining us had been such that our establishment was all that stood between her and the gaol system.

She already understood that a visit to my study would mean a caning, and admitted that she'd been caned once before. "How many strokes did you receive on that occasion?" "Twelve, sir." I'd, needless to say, bear that in mind when determining her punishment.

"Please remove your skirt and hand it to Miss Temple.... Neatly!" And then, to Miss Grey's apparent mortification, came the instruction to remove her knickers and then to bend over the desk. I could then complete my own preparations: jacket off, cufflink removed, shirt sleeve rolled up, (senior) cane selected from the stand. A quick hand spanking followed to warm the bent-over girl up as much as I ever do whilst trying to maintain a degree of authenticity in the (very unauthentic!) scene!

She'd confessed to a dozen strokes as her previous punishment, so that was clearly the starting point for what followed. A very conventional caning, this, done by the book: each whack administered hard, a "thank you, sir" afterwards, a ten or twenty second pause to let the impact of the stroke sink it. The weals rising on Miss Grey's backside were most impressive; she was gasping at the hardest strokes, but taking her thrashing very bravely and valiantly.

After the twelfth, I informed the young lady that she would receive six more – but that she didn't need to count these. I administered them hard, in quick succession, and the punishment was over. I lectured her as I re-adjusted my shirt, threading my cufflink back into position, before making her stand and sort out her own clothing. And then, after a final few words from me and a final defiant glance from Miss Grey, Miss Temple escorted the young lady on her way and the door shut behind them...

Canings in the country house

By Abel on 10 November 2009

Whilst most of the disciplinarians imagined in my little fantasies are male, there's always space for the occasional strict female. The stern Headmistress, summoning a girl to her study; the prison officer stripping a reluctant girl before applying a birching; the mistress of the house dealing with the maids.

The final case sparked interesting thoughts of a young woman, recently married to a grand Duke. Disciplining the female staff, he'd explain, was to be one of her responsibilities; he'd provide her with a cane, encourage her to practice on the cushions, and inform her that the butler would be standing by to cut birch rods should she have to deal with a more serious offence.

Only, she'd flinch from her duties – memories of being chastised by her own father mixing with a desire to be liked, loved even, by the staff. Particularly the pretty young thing who was her own lady's maid, her dresser – her confidant, even, in this scary, lonely big house.

The day would come, inevitably, when her favourite made some heinous mistake. The Duke, over dinner, would check with his wife: "You will be caning her later, I assume?" Trembling, she'd confirm that she would – and trembling again the following morning at breakfast, she would confirm that she had.

Only, you see, she hadn't. She'd called the girl into her dressing room, scolded her, and sent her on her way.

Who knows how the Duke would discover her deceit – the trusted butler, listening at the door, noting the absence of whacking inside? But both his elegant young wife and her favoured maid would be called into his study.

"I understand that my wife let you off with a scolding," he'd inform the girl. "It might have been better for you had she carried out her duties." He'd make her lift her skirts; bare herself; give her a dozen of the harshest cuts; send her on her way.

And then he'd turn to his new wife. "Clearly it's not only the staff who need discipline," he'd comment disapprovingly, before instructing her to adopt the position recently vacated by her maid. Twelve more strokes would echo out, teaching her an important lesson that would not be quickly forgotten, before holding her tight in his arms.

The school trip

By Abel on 18 November 2009

A party of girls on a trip to another school, requiring a night away. A big sports match, a tournament of some description, perhaps?

A group of the young ladies – four, five of them? – are caught misbehaving by their hosts. They're called before the master who's supervising the trip.

He expresses his disappointment in them, and takes out the cane. Two strokes each, on the hand, bringing tears to their eyes and heartfelt apologies.

And then the last girl stands before him. A girl he likes – one he tutors, is ever-so-close to, without ever crossing lines that shouldn't be crossed between a master and a pupil. A girl who is rather – maybe rather too – fond of him.

But he can't cane her. "The rules are clear. Only the headmaster may cane prefects. I'll have to report you to him on our return tomorrow."

And she pleads, and he eventually relents. "I understand that the prefects receive six of the best, on the bare?"

"Yes, sir."

And so he makes her bend over. And explains that, as he only has a junior cane and the headmaster uses the senior rattan on the prefects, he's going to double the number of strokes...

Afterwards, she cries. Apologises. Thanks him for not sending her to the headmaster. Standing close to him, leans her face against his chest, dampening his shirt with her tears. And feels safe in his tight, re-assuring hug.

The suffragette

By Abel on 24 November 2009

It was an awkward gathering late that evening in the drawing room of the grand London townhouse: the gentleman, his niece, the police inspector.

The girl, aged seventeen, had been missing all day. Panic had ensued; her absence had been reported, searches undertaken. They'd found her, eventually – in the cell of a police station, amidst the other protestors they'd arrested earlier.

"Wilful vandalism", the inspector called it – daubing messages demanding equality on the walls of public buildings across the capital. "They want equality?" he continued: "They should be birched, then." But, thanks to the gentleman's friends in high places, no charges would be brought against this particular young lady – this time.

The gentleman raised his hand to silence the officer: "Thank you for your help, inspector, and for your advice. I shall take matters into my own hands from here." He rang a bell; the butler appeared. "Thomson here will show you the way out."

When they were alone, he turned to the girl. "I shall see you in your bedroom in twenty minutes' time," he told her. "Go and get ready for bed."

She mounted the stairs, half in anger ("I was doing what was right"), half in dread. He was a kind man: he'd been good to her since he'd taken her in. But she knew what happened when he sent her upstairs like this. And, she had to admit, she'd deserved the two whippings he'd had to give her. But her righteous fury made the thought of bending over, of taking the harsh strokes with his crop, even worse.

She was washed and in her nightdress by the time he arrived. She started to protest: "It's not fair. We should have the vote. You can't punish me for trying to change the system when it's wrong."

And he listened, and sat next to her on the bed, and agreed. He confided in her: he knew the ringleaders, was active behind the scenes lobbying on their behalf. If she wanted to protest, he was proud of her.

"But," he added, "that doesn't excuse you leaving the house without permission today, or the worry you've caused us. We've been beside ourselves dreading what might have become of you."

She nodded sadly. And when he told her that he was going to put her over his knee and spank her, she was almost grateful for the chance to make amends – not for her protest, but for hurting those who cared about her.

The workhouse benefactor

By Abel on 25 November 2009

To a Victorian workhouse as I slept last night. A benefactor was visiting – a youngish gentleman, who'd recently inherited his father's title and estate and was therefore on the lookout for new staff.

Six of the best girls were lined up for him to inspect; they'd been scrubbed and dressed in clean clothes before his arrival, and ordered to be on their very best behaviour. He talked kindly to them – asking how long they'd been in the establishment, whether they'd been well-treated, what they wanted to do with their lives.

Each girl answered politely, save for the last. She initially refused to answer, then – when pressed – spoke up vehemently. "What do you care? You know nothing of what life's really like. You swan in here in your fine clothes, looking for cheap labour to exploit. And in return you expect us to bow down and worship you?"

The governor, of course, sent an underling to fetch a birch; the girl was tied over a chair, and six smart strokes applied. After she'd been punished, she was told to apologise to the visitor – but refused.

"It appears, governor, that you may not have punished her with sufficient vigour. May I?" And the young gentleman removed his jacket, rolled up the sleeve of his shirt and took the birch. The girl was tied down once more; her second flogging, incomparably harder, soon had her pleading for forgiveness and mercy.

Afterwards, she stood before him, attempting not to let him see her cry, trying to avoid his eyes. "I'll take this one, governor, if I may," the gentleman requested. "I like a girl with spirit – and she can be taught good manners."

(The dream then degenerated into a Mills and Boon romance: master and servant became close; a check through the workhouse paperwork revealed that she'd been abandoned as a baby by a rich family fallen on hard times; they were therefore able to marry. All extremely improbable – whereas the birching scene, of course, was entirely realistic!)

Pre-Christmas spankings
By Abel on 30 November 2009

They were setting up the Christmas market in Stuttgart last Tuesday evening as I wandered around the city centre. Craft shops of every description mingled with stalls selling beautiful Christmas decorations; highly-decorated wooden booths offered bratwurst and beer.

Right in the middle of the central square was the most ornate of the structures, around which snaked a long line of young ladies. My German is a little rusty these days, but it's still good enough for me to have deciphered the neatly written notice – as if the body language of those in the queue, and the pained looks on the faces of those emerging weren't enough to give it away:

> Girls! Been naughty this year? Worried that Father Frost won't visit? Come inside and have your misbehaviour dealt with! You know you'll be on the receiving end one way or the other this festive season. Paddle or presents? The choice is yours!

I broke my penis
By Abel on 3 December 2009

Well, *that* was an interesting evening...

See, Cath and I headed out yesterday afternoon to a local antique shop yesterday, and found that it stocked a rather nice selection of riding crops. I studied a few and made my selection, at which point the elderly gentleman chatting to the owner turned to me and said, "You know what that is, don't you? A bull's manhood."

For, indeed, I had managed to buy a prized artefact – a pizzle. I defer to the authoritative "Agony & Ecstacy" for more details:

> The pizzle is a whip made from a bull's penis (which is also called a pizzle)... The penis is cleaned, salted and dried. By stretching and sometimes twisting during this process, it becomes a highly flexible rod-like whip of 3ft overall length (actually, it can be stretched much longer, becoming increasingly thin).

They describe it as a' severe' implement, noting that the eighteenth-century German equivalent, the Ochenziemer, "was used as a harsher alternative to the birch rod for judiciary punishments":

> If mentioned in the sentence, the lashes were given during the culprit stay at the prison. The men usually got it on the bare back, tied to a post, the women on mostly on clothed buttocks, frequently covered only with thin wet pants but sometimes also on the bare, while lying on a long low bench which had restraining mechanisms for holding the head and feet.

But even when a flogging was not included in the judge's sentence, the pizzle (or a birch rod) was used for the customary "welcome" and "farewell" floggings given to all prisoners, male and female, just after entering and just before leaving the prison. Those floggings were usually given in front of people, both women and men, that went to prison just for watching (and enjoying) the punishments.

So what of my newly-acquired penis? Well, as night fell I became the master of the local hunt. Young

Catherine was a maid in the house of one of the other huntsmen; she'd managed to get in the way of the hunt that afternoon, and a flogging was called for – for endangering herself, the riders and the horses.

The master took out his most feared implement – the pizzle – and bade her bare herself and bend over. By her eighteenth and final stroke, the sorry young lady was pleading for forgiveness... as was my lovely new possession, the leather tip of which managed to fly off during the flogging!

I asked young Catherine, once the maid had been dismissed, to tell me how the pizzle compared to other riding crops she'd experienced. "I don't think I ever have," she foolishly replied, so a selection of five were duly brought out and tested in turn. After four strokes of each, the dressage whip was voted the winner, if you're wondering!

Demonstrating their submission

By Abel on 7 December 2009

See, I think most noblemen let their subjects off too easily. What's all this paying of tithes and droit de seigneur, if there's no good whippings going on?

The duke in a recent dream had a better scheme, whereby the folks of his fiefdom were forced to demonstrate their loyalty and submission to him in a traditional ceremony once a year. Each village was required to send him one of their maidens; once the girls were gathered in the great hall, they'd be stripped and led to the field below the castle walls. There, they'd be tied to posts – and each would be soundly flogged in turn.

A great banquet would follow for all of those present, albeit the girls who'd just been whipped rarely had much appetite for the feast.

Legal remedies

By Abel on 11 December 2009

My team at work has been working lately on contracts for our business. We've hired a posh lawyer to draft the agreements, and we've been merrily (?!) ploughing through them, checking clause-by-clause.

One particular topic provoked a little debate, so a colleague decided to Google the issue concerned. And, lo and behold, he discovered that the very same document that we were reviewing (prepared for us at considerable cost by the lawyer) was freely available on the web.

Needless to say, complaints will follow. Now, the "File Properties" in Microsoft Word shows that the document was created by a lady called Patricia. And, as my wife pointed out, young Trish might end up in rather serious trouble.

As the most junior lawyer on the books, newly-qualified, she'd have been rushed off her feet. Rather than miss a deadline for drafting our document, she'd resorted to the quickest means she knew and copied it from the internet.

The matter will be dealt by her superiors with under "Any Other Business" at next week's partners meeting. She'll be called in and lectured on her conduct, before being punished: knickers down, skirt lifted, bent over the boardroom table whilst the senior partner administers the twelve strokes that would serve as her final warning.

Kitchen implement of doom

By Haron on 13 December 2009

Abel called me from the kitchen in his "I'm about to smack you" voice. When I arrived, I saw that he was grinning from ear to ear, and also that he was hiding something behind his back. "Bend over," he said, very pleased with himself. "Hands on your knees."

I obeyed. Something invisible swung up and cracked down, leaving quite intense, not unpleasant sting. "Ow?" I asked.

Another two strokes, in quick succession. This time I yelped with more conviction. "Very good," said Abel. "You can stand up. Do you like my new implement?"

And he produced from behind his back the single least romantic kitchen pervertible my bottom has ever encountered. Any guesses what it was?

Don't bother trying, I'll tell you. It was an empty tube from a roll of baking foil!!!

Some things make excellent spanking implements, but must, nevertheless, never ever be used as such. Ever.

Escaping from slavery

By Haron on 18 December 2009

A few nights ago I had a dream with a very complex plot, revolving around a medium-sized island close enough to England to be seen with the naked eye, and yet out of the British jurisdiction. This was where slaves were kept. If you were somehow politically undesirable – a migrant, a petty criminal, "underserving poor" – you were sent to this island to work for the rest of your life.

I was a slave too. For most of the dream, I was preoccupied with escape. I would run off to get onto a boat, get caught, get beaten; I would try to swim the channel, get caught, get beaten. Once I made it all the way to the shore, only to be immediately identified as a slave, because I cowered from figures of authority.

A lot of punishment can fit into a dream. Mostly it was done by having me tied to a wooden post, with rope looped through a metal ring at its top. I'd be whipped with a wide leather strap – on my bottom, across my back. It being a dream, the whippings didn't hurt, but they brought me so much anguish that I thought they did.

In the end, I did escape. I flew away.

Cruel to be kind

By Abel on 31 December 2009

A week or so back, a new twist to a much-loved old fantasy came to mind: the one concerning a young nobleman and his favourite maid – where the boundaries of the master-servant relationship strain in the context of an always-chaste, yet ever-so-close rapport.

This particular lass had been guilty of the utmost carelessness, having set fire to an expensive tapestry in his lordship's room. Fortunately, the flames had been put out before the building itself caught light – but the tapestry itself was still ruined. Yet he – seeing how mortified she was by her mistake, how tearful, how repentant, and simply wanting to hug her and tell her that everything was fine – was prepared to let the matter go without further discussion.

However, word reached the nobleman's father, a Duke no less, of the disaster that had nearly taken place. The older gentleman's carriage soon arrived at his son's door;

a debate ensued; agreement was reached, the maid was summoned.

The matter could not go unpunished, the duke would inform her, no matter how impeccable her previous service. The butler had been ordered to send one of his men to the woods, to cut the switches that would be bound into the birch. Once that was done, his son would punish her. Because of her past good conduct, her birching would take place in private, and would only comprise twenty strokes across her bare bottom rather than the fifty the duke had initially requested. But he would personally inspect her after she'd been whipped and, should he feel that she had been chastised too lightly by his son, he would personally administer the additional thirty with the utmost severity...

Clearly, the younger gentleman would have no choice but to inflict the twenty strokes as hard as he could, despite his feelings for the girl, to save her from further punishment. And then, later, once his father had inspected her, he'd be able to give her a much-needed hugs.

Only – and rarely for me – the same scenario popped into my mind for a second time as I slept a couple of nights later. Only on this occasion, the Duke demonstrated a particularly cruel streak – determining that, despite the evident effectiveness of the maid's initial flogging, she did indeed deserve more.

The butler was despatched for a fresh birch, and asked to tie the girl over a table. Her additional, agonising thirty duly followed – as, then, did comfort for her behind his young lordship's bedroom door, which remained firmly locked so he could take care of her until the following morning...

Here's hoping your spanking dreams come true in 2010...

Abel and Haron are a kinky married couple, living in the UK. Both are published authors of award-winning erotica. Active in the fetish scene, they are both enthusiastic spanking role-players, with kinky thoughts rarely far from their respective imaginations.

Abel's 42 (and is the one who does the spanking), Haron's 30 (and she still gets asked for ID when buying alcohol!)

The Spanking Writers is well established as one of the web's most highly acclaimed literary spanking sites. This second "best of" volume brings together the most popular posts from the years 2008-2009.

Ideal bedside reading for fans of the cane, tawse, birch and paddle; perfect if your kinky interests embrace punished maids, disciplined schoolgirls and whipped miscreants.

Whether you're interested in historical spankings, fetish fantasies or real-life corporal punishment scenes, "The Spanking Writers" will entertain and stimulate.

"The Spanking Writers" can be found online at www.spankingwriters.com/blog.

www.ingramcontent.com/pod-product-compliance
Ingram Content Group UK Ltd.
Pitfield, Milton Keynes, MK11 3LW, UK
UKHW041438180426
11947UKWH00007B/511